Dictionary of Information Communication Technology (ICT)

DICTIONARY
OF
INFORMATION COMMUNICATION TECHNOLOGY (ICT)

ISMAIL THAMARASSERI
Lecturer in Education
Farook B.Ed. College Kottakkal
Parappur, Kerala

KANISHKA PUBLISHERS, DISTRIBUTORS
NEW DELHI-110 002

KANISHKA PUBLISHERS, DISTRIBUTORS
4697/5-21A, Ansari Road, Daryaganj
New Delhi -110 002
Phones : 2327 0497, 2328 8285
Fax : 011-2328 8285
E-mail : kanishka_publishing@yahoo.co.in

Dictionary of Information Communication Technology (ICT)
Edition-2014

PRINTED IN INDIA

Published by Madan Sachdeva for Kanishka Publishers, Distributors, 4697/5-21A, Ansari Road, Daryaganj, New Delhi-110 002, Typeset by Sunshine Graphics, Delhi, and Printed at Rajdhani Printers, Delhi.

PREFACE

The ICT Dictionary a reference containing descriptions of terms related to ICT. Its primary aim is to provide the readers clear and authentic definition of computer-related terms and ICT terminologies. Besides this it will be highly helpful reference guide to all people form different walks of life.

The dictionary is a comprehensive treatment of digital communication,. computer networking, information and communication technology, phrases and concepts of this rapidly growing field. It is intended for students, teachers, professionals and all those who are genuinely interested in understanding ICT.

The editor extremely indebted to various authors, editors, educationists, technologists, research scholars, whose views and opinions have been incorporated in the Dictionary. The editor grateful to his colleagues, friends, family members and students whose offered suggestions, guidance and assistance. The editor also wish to express thanks to M/s. Infratec Computer Systems, Calicut University for the computerization of the great work.

Finally, the editor whole heartedly expresses his indebtedness to M/s. *Kanishka Publishers, Distributors*, New Delhi for the meticulous process and publishing of the work. Moreover all the suggestions and comments are invited for the further improvement of the work.

ISMAIL THAMARASSERI

A

AAL5 (ATM Adaptation Layer 5): The protocol an application uses to send data over an ATM network. AALF, which is part of the ATM stack, accepts and delivers large packets of data (up to 64K bytes).

Abacus: The earliest known computing device in which beads are moved along wires set in a wooden frame.

Abel: Advanced Boolean Expression Language; a software compiler language for SPLD programming; a type of hardware description language (HDSL).

ABR (Available Bit Rate): A type of service offered by ATM.

Access: Reaching and obtaining the desired data.

Access Control: Deals with the policies and mech-anisms to prohibit a user/process from accessing those resources/information, which he/she/it is not authorized to access.

Access Delay: The time network interface waits before it can access a shared network.

Access Time: The time interval between the instant at which information is called from the storage and instant at which delivery is completed.

Accumulator: A special register in the central processor in which a number can be temporarily stored during arithmetic calculations.

Accumulator Register (A): A register, which holds the initial data to operated, upon, the intermediate results, and also the final results of processing operations.

ACK (Acknowledgement): A short returned to inform a sender that data has arrived at its intended destination.

ACL (Access Control List): A security mechanism that specifies users or computer programmes that can access a particular object.

Acronym: A word formed from the first letters of the words in a phrase or sentence.

Active Document: A World Wide Web document that is a computer programme. After downloading an active document, the browser runs the programme on the user's computer. The active document can change the display continuously. See dynamic document, static document, and URL.

Active Hub: The central hub in a network the retransmits the data it receives and can be connected to computers or to other hubs.

Activity Ratio: The ratio of the total number of records in transaction file and the total number of records in master file.

ADA: A high-level programming language.

Adaptive Retransmission: The ability of a transport protocol to change its retransmission timer continuously to accommodate variations in internet delay. TCP is the best known protocol that uses adaptive retransmission.

Addend: In addition, the number that is added to another number called the augend.

Adder: The electronic circuitry in a computer that carries out arithmetic and logical operations.

Address: A unique reference given to each word in the central processor memory or each sector in a direct access backing storage device.

Address Bus: Generally, a one-way group of conductors from the microprocessor to memory, containing address information.

Address Mask: A 32-bit value that specifies how an IP address is divided into network and host portions. Address bits not covered by the mask correspond to the host portion. Also called a subnet mask.

Address Register: A local storage register, which contains the address of the next instruction to be executed.

Address Resolution: The mapping from one address to another, usually from a high-level address (e.g., an IP address) to a low-level address (e.g., and Ethernet address).

Address Resolution Protocol (ARP): A protocol in the TCP/IP suite that correlates logical network addresses with physical addresses.

Adjacency: Characteristic of cells in a Kamaugh map in which there is a single-variable change from one cell to another cell next to it on any of its four sides.

ADSL (Asymmetric Digital Subscriber Line): A technology to deliver digital information at high-speed over the same twisted pair wiring used to deliver telephone service. The downstream bit rate is higher than the upstream rate because most subscribers retrieve much more information than they send. See HDSL.

Algebraic Language: A language whose statements resemble the algebraic expressions, as for example, Algol, Fortran.

Algol: A computer language standardized by an international committee (Algorithmic language). It was mainly used to programme numerial applications. It is extinct.

Algorithm: A kind of scheme that narrates the point-to-point evolution of the technique to deal with the solution of a particular task such as flow chart dealing with programme procedure.

Alignment: Process of organizing and fixing the position and order of words and lines in a document.

Alphabetic: Pertaining to a character set, which contains the letters A to Z and the blank character.

Alphabetic Character: A letter from the set (A-Z).

Alphameric Characters: All the characters A-Z, digits 0-9 and special symbols.

Alphanumeric: Pertaining to a character set, which contains letters, digits, and usually other special characters, such as comma, dollar sign, plus sigh, etc.

Alphanumeric Characters : See alphameric.

ALU: Arithmetic and logical unit which performs arithmetic and logical operations.

American National Standard Institute (ANSI): A.U.S. based national organization, which establishes uniform standards in several fields.

American Standard Code for Information Interchange (ASCII): A standard coding system for computers. ASCII-7 is a 7-bit code, and its extended version, ASCII-8, is an 8-bit code.

Amplitude: In a pulse waveform, the height or maximum value of the pulse as measured from its low level.

Analog: A signal transmission technology used on broad-band networks. This type of signal creates analog wavforms from digital data for transmission and requires a digital-to-analog converter (d-to-a) to reverse the conversion. A device called an analog-go-digital converter is required to convert the signal back into digital data.

Analog Channel: A communication path used for transmitting and receiving continuously varying electrical signals.

Analog Computer : A computer, which operates on data, which is in the form of continuously variable physical quantities, such as electrical current.

Analog-to-digital Converter (ADC): A device used to convert an analog signal to sequence of digital codes.

Analytical Engine: Mechanical calculating machine developed by Charles Babbage in 1833. It is considered as the proto type of computer.

And: Term used in BASIC for carrying out the logical operation of combining two bits.

AND: A basic logic operation in which a true (HIGH) output occurs only if all the input conditions are true (HIGH).

AND Gate: A logic gate that produces a HIGH output only when all the inputs are HIGH.

Android: A root which looks like a human being.

Angel: Someone who invests his or her own money in a start-up.

Animation: A display of sequence of drawing which gives impression as if the object is moving.

Anonymous FTP: Access to an FTP server using the login name *anonymous* and the password *guest*. Not all FTP servers permit anonymous FTP.

Anonymous FTP Site: On the internet, a computer, which allows a user to log in with a username of anonymous and then a password, which is the user's e-mail address.

ANSI: American National Standards Institute.

Antivirus: The programme (like Norton, PC-Cillin, McAfee, etc.) which scans files to detect, repair virus-infected programmes and safeguard against viruses.

Antivirus Utility: A programme to cure a computer from virus infection.

APCM (Adaptive Pulse Code Modulation): A scheme for digital encoding of audio in which successive values represent differences in the sampled wave instead of absolute value. See PCM.

API (Application Programme Interface): A generic reference to a set of procedures that an application programme uses to access a service. A network API consists of procedures a programme uses to access protocol software; the most well-known is the socket API.

APL: Acronym for A Programming Language.

Apple Talk: An old set of network protocols developed and sold by Apple Computer Corporation.

Applet: A computer programme that forms the central part of an active World Wide Web document. An applet is written in a programming language such as Java.

Application Layer: The uppermost layer of the OSI Reference Model for networking. This layer provides a consistent interface to the network for all computer software. The interface is commonly referred to as an Application Programming Interface (API), which allows for a programme to be written once, without regard to the type of network involved, and then used on any network, regardless of the protocol in use.

Application Programmer: A programmer who prepares application software.

Application Programming Interface (API): The building blocks for software applications, which include routines, protocols, and tools.

Application Software: A set of one or more programmes designed to solve a specific problem or do a specific task, such as pay calculation, processing of examination results, stores accounting and inventory control, etc.

Application-layer Gateway: A programme that acts as proxy to provide service indirectly. Application gateways are used in Internet firewalls to allow employees in an organization to access the internet according to the organization's security policy.

Architecture: The terminal functional arrangement of the elements that give a device its particular operating characteristics.

Archiving: The process of storing old data files on separate disk or tapes to make room for new files on the hard disk of a computer.

Area: An OSPF term for a set of routers that use OSPF to exchange link-status information.

Argument: A constant, variable or string variable from which a function determines its values.

Arithmetic Logic Unit (ALU): The unit of a computing system, which performs all mathematical and logical operations. It is one of the components of the Central Processing Unit (CPU) of the computer.

ARP (Address Resolution Protocol): The protocol in a computer uses to map an IP address into a hardware address. A computer that invokes ARP broadcasts a request to the target which computer replies.

Arpanet: Advanced Research Project Agency Network; a computer network which proceeded the Internet.

Array: In PLD, a matrix formed by rows of product-term lines and columns of input lines with a programmable cell at each junction.

Arrow Keys: The four keys in the Key Board which move the cursor up and down and to the left and right.

Artificial Intelligence: A branch of computer science, which deals with computers, which possess reasoning, learning, and thinking capabilities that resemble those of humans.

AS (Autonomous System): A group of network and routers has under one administrative authority. For routing purposes, the Internet is divided into Autonomous Systems.

ASCII (American Standard Code for Information Interchange): A standard that assigns unique values to 128 characters, including upper and lower. A standard that assigns unique values to 128 characters, including upper and lower case letters, digits, punctuation, and control characters. Details can be found in Appendix 2. See EBCDIC.

ASN.1 (Abstract Syntax Notation-1): A standard for represen-ting data. The SNMP protocol uses ASN. 1 to represent object names.

ASP (Active Server Pages): A dynamic Web page technology is closely linked to Microsoft's Web server. The server interprets Visual Basic code that is embedded in each page whenever the pages are requested.

Assembler: A computer programme, which translates an assembly language programme to its machine language programme to its machine language equivalent.

Assembly Language: A programming language, which allows instructions and storage location to be represented by letters and symbols instead of numbers. Also known as symbolic language.

Assembly Programme: A programme written in an assembly language. Also known as symbolic programme.

Assess Time: The time from the application of a valid memory address to the appearance of valid output data.

Assign Button: The button for selecting options from the dialog box of OPEN OFFICE IMPRESS and to use them in text or image.

Associative Law: In addition (ORing) and multiplication (ANDing) of three or more variables, the order in which the variables are grouped makes no difference.

Asynchronous: Characteristic of any communication system in which the sender can transmit data without warning. The receiver must be prepared to accept data at any time. See synchronous.

Asynchronous Communication: Data transmission mode in which the sender can send data at any convenient time and the receiver will accept it.

Asynchronous Counter: A type of counter in which each stage is clocked from the output of the proceeding stage.

Asynchronous Transfer Mode (ATM): A networking technology based on the transfer of fixed-size packets, or cells. The fixed size of the cells stabilizes transmission, which is especially useful for large transmissions such as video or audio data.

Asynchrounous: Having no fixed time relationship; not occurring at the same time.

Attenuation: The weakening of a signal as it is transferred across a communications medium.

Augend: In addition, the number to which the addend is added.

AUI (Attachment Unit Interface): The type of connector used with the original, thick wire Ethernet.

Auto Correct: A feature of a programme that automatically corrects spelling.

Automated tape library: A mass storage device, which uses a set of magnetic tapes and tape drives with a controller mounted in a single unit. All the tapes of an automated tape library form a single large storage unit. They are typically used for data archiving and as an online data backup device for automated backup.

Automatic Teller Machine (ATM): An unattended machine used in banks, which allows a customer to deposit or withdraw cash by the use of an electronic card without the need to interact with a bank employee.

Autonegotiation: The mechanism that a 10/100 Ethernet port uses to detect the maximum speed of a computer.

Auxiliary: Storage other than the main memory unit. Also called secondary or external storage.

Auxiliary Memory: A storage, which supplements the main memory of a computer. Often referred to as secondary storage, this section of the computer's memory is non-volatile and has low cost per bit stored, but it generally has an operating speed far slower than that of the primary storage.

Availability: The percentage of time that a computer is operational.

AWT (Abstract Window Toolkit): A library of graphics procedures used with the Java language to manipulate windows on a bit-mapped display. At various times, the designers have expanded AWT to Alternative Window Toolkit and Applet Widget Toolkit.

B

B Channel (Bearer Channel): The term telephone companies is used to denote a channel configured to handle a voice telephone circuit. ISDN includes B channel service. See D channel.

Back Space: Key that moves the cursor on place to the left, erasing the character.

Backbone: The main trunk lines of a computer network, which facilitates the interconnection of the computers and networks on the same network.

Background Processing: The automatic execution of lower-priority (background) computer programmes, when higher-priority (foreground) programmes are not using the system resources.

Backing Storage: Storage that is located out-side the central processor but connected to it electrically, and through which data can be transferred to an from the processor. Information stored by the computer on magnetic disks, tapes, etc.

Backup: Alternative facilities of programmes, data files, hardware equipment, etc., which are used in case the original one is destroyed, lost, or fails to operate.

Backup File: A copy of a file, created as a safety precaution against loss of data caused due to corruption, or inadvertent deletion of the original file.

Band Printers: See chain printers.

Bandwidth: The range of frequencies available for data transmission. The wider the bandwidth of a communications system, the more data it can transmit in a given period of time.

Banner: A graphic image used on a Website as an advertisement; the information superhighway's version of billboards.

Bar Code: A pattern of printed lines in binary coding that can be read into a computer by light pen scanning.

Bar Codes: Representation of alphanumeric data by a combination of adjacent vertical lines (called bards) by varying their width and the spacing between them. A *barcode reader* is scanner, which is used for reading (decoding) bar-coded data.

Base: The total number of digits (symbols) available to represent numbers in a positional number system.

1000BaseT: The technical name for gigabit Ethernet.

100BaseT: The technical name for fast Ethernet (100Mbps).

10Base 2: 802.3 Ethernet on thin coaxial cable. The 10 specifies a bandwidth of 10 Mbps, the Base specifies that it's a baseband transmission, and the 2 indicates a maximum segment length for this cable type of 200m (the actual limitation is 185).

10Base 5: 802.3 Ethernet on thick coaxial cable. The 10 specifies a bandwidth of 10Mbps, the Base indicates that it's a baseband transmission, and the 5 indicates a maximum segment length for this cable type of 500m.

10BaseT: The technical name for 10 Mbps twisted pair Ethernet.

Baseband Technology: The term used to describe a networking technology that uses a small part of the electromagnetic spectrum and sends only one signal at a time over the underlying medium. Most LANs use baseband signaling (e.g., Ethernet and FDDI). See broad-band technology.

Baseline: A network's normal performance measurements over time that can be used to diagnose or troubleshoot network problems.

BASIC: Beginner's All-Purpose Symbolic Instruction Code; a programming language.

Basic Statement: The unit of a BASIC programme. In BASIC, each instruction given to the computer is a statement.

Batch Mode: User/application programmes run on the computer, one at a time.

Batch Operating System: A system programme which facilitates the execution of a series of user programmes without any manual intervention.

Batch Processing: The running of several computer programmes one after another without the need of a human operator to run each programme individually.

Baud: A unit for measuring data transmission speed. It is used to describe the capacity of a carrier. In general usage, a baud is identical to bits per second.

BCD: Binary coded decimal; a digital code in which each of the decimal digits, 0, through 9, is represented by a group of four bits.

2B+D service: An ISDN service that includes two standard telephone connections plus a data connection.

BEDO DRAM: Burst extended data output dynamic random-access memory.

Beginners All-Purpose Symbolic Instruction Code (BASIC): An easy-to-learn, high-level, interactive programming language, which is frequently used with personal computers, and timesharing environment.

Bernoulli Disk: A magnetic disk-based storage medium in which a single hard disk platter is encased in a plastic cartridge.

Best-effort: Characteristic of any network system that makes a best attempt to deliver data, but does not guarantee delivery. Many networks sue the best-effort approach.

Beta Site: A test site, usually erected in the authoring phase of a Website.

Beta Testing: The use of beta version of a software by a selected set of users for identifying errors, which might have been overlooked during the regular testing phase.

Beta Version: The version of a software, which is released to a selected set of users for testing, before it actual release.

BGP (Border Gateway Protocol): The main Exterior Gateway Protocol used in the Internet. BGP provides routing among Autonomous Systems.

Bidding: A technique protocols use for dynamic address configuration. A computer selects an address at random, and broadcasts a message to determine whether the address is in use. Alternative scheme use servers top manage addresses. See DHCP.

Bidirectional: Having two directions. In a bidreictional shift register, the stored data can be shifted right or left.

Binary: A number system having a radix of two and using two digits only – '0' or '1'. It is the smallest unit of information. Bit is the short form for the words 'binary digit'.

Binary Coded Decimal: A representation of decimal digits which uses a unique string of 4 bits to represent each digit.

Binary Coded Decimal (BCD): One of the early coding systems, which is based on the idea of converting each digit of a decimal number into its binary equivalent, rather than converting the entire decimal value into a pure binary form. For example, the decimal number 42 is represented by 0100 0010 in 8-4-2-1 BCD notation.

Binary Digits: Either the character 0 or 1, the digits in the binary numeral system.

Binary Exponential Backoff: The scheme used by computers on an Ethernet following a collision. Each computer doubles the time it waits after each successive collision.

Binary Number System: A number system with a base of two. It consists of two digits: 0 and 1.

Binary Sequence: Binary numbers occurring in order.

Bind: The name of a popular programme that implements Domain Name Server functionality.

Biometric Device: A device used for user authentication, which verifies some physical characteristic of a user, such as the person's appearance, fingerprints, had geometry, voice, or signature.

BIOS: Basic input/output system; a set of programmes in ROM that interfaces the I/O devices in a computer system.

Bipolar: Having two opposite charge carries within the transistor structure.

Bistable: Having two stable stats. Flip-flops and latches are bistable multivibrators.

Bit: Acronym for binary digit, which stands for one binary piece of information. This can be either 0 or 1.

Bit Time: The interval of time occupied by a single bit in a sequence of bits; the period of the clock.

Bitmap: A method of displaying graphic images on a monitor by altering the colour (or turning on or off) of individual dots (pixels) on the coordinate system.

BJT: Bipolar junction transistor; a seminconductor device used for switching or amplification. A BJT has two junctions, the base-emitter junction and the base-collect junction.

Black Box: An expression for the processor and memory.

Blank Presentation: An empty square space in the software to prepare display slides.

Block: A group of related items (records, characters, etc.) handled as a unit during input and output. A section of programme code treated as a unit.

Blocking Factor: The process of grouping two or more records together to form a block, and the number of records put together in each block is called a blocking factor.

Bluetooth: A wireless networkign technology used for short distance (e.g., to connect a wireless mouse to a computer).

BMP: Abbreviation of Bitmap. A common format for graphics. A file name extension.

BNC Connector: The type of connector used with thin wire Ethernet.

BNF: Backus Naur Form is a notation used to precisely define syntax rules of a programming language.

Bold: To display of print the text more darkly.

Boolean Addition: In Boolean algebra, the OR operation.

Boolean Algebra: An algebra, which deals with logical propositions, which are either true or false. This algebra is suitable for use with binary number system, and is very useful in designing logic circuits, which are used by the processors of computer systems.

Boolean Expression: An expression of variables and operators used to express the operation of a logic circuit.

Boolean Function: A mathematical function in Boolean algebra. For example, $w = x + Y.z$.

Boolean Multiplication: In Boolean algebra, the AND operation.

Boolean Variable: A variable used in Boolean algebra. It can assume a value or false.

Boot Strap: The process used to set up a programme once the system is operational.

Booting: To start or restart a computer system by loading of the operating system into the main memory of the computer.

BOOTP (BOOT Strap Protocol): A protocol that a computer uses when it first starts to obtain information needed to configure the protocol software. BOOTP uses IP and UDP to broadcast a request and receive a response before IP has been completely configured.

Border Gateway Protocol (BGP): A part of the TCP/IP protocol suite that enables communication of routing information between routers.

Bot: A robot, or programme, that automatically does specified tasks.

bps (bits per second): The rate at which data can be transmitted across a network. The number of bits per second may differ from the baud rate because more than one bit can be encoded in a single baud. See Gbps, Kbps, and Mbps.

Branch Instruction: An instruction, which transfers programme control to a non-consecutive instruction.

BRI (Basic Rate Interface): The ISDN service that provides two B channels plus a data channel. BRI is suitable for small businesses. See PRI.

Bricks and Motor (B&M): A term describing traditional business made of bricks and mortar rather than the byes of cyber business.

Bridge: A hardware device that connects two LAN segments and copies frames from one to the other. Most bridge hardware uses physical addresses to learn which computers attach to which segments so the bridge can avoid copying frames unless needed.

Broadband: A signal transmission technology for transferring analog signals along multiple channels of a communications medium simultaneously.

Broadband Channel: Communication channels, which are capable of data transfer rates of 1 million baud (bits/second) or more. They are used to handle high volumes of data, and for high-speed computer to computer communication, or for simultaneous transmission of data to several devices.

Broadband Technology: The term used to describe a networking technology that uses a large part of the electromagnetic spectrum to achieve higher throughput rates. Usually broadband systems employ frequency division multiplexing to allow multiple, independent communications to proceed simultaneously over a single underlying medium. See baseband technology.

Broadcast: A form of delivery in which one copy of a packet is delivered to each computer on a network. See cluster, multicast, and unicast.

Broadcast Address: A special address that causes the underlying system to delivery a copy of a packet to all computers on a network.

Broadcast Satellite: A network system in which a satellite broadcasts all packets and allows individual receivers to discard packets intended for other recipients.

Browse: Searching for data in an Online system or database.

Browser: A software tool, which provides several navigation facilities to help users do internet surfing easily and effectively.

Brush Selection Tool: A tool in graphic software to select brushes of different types and shapes.

Bubble Sort: A sorting procedure which 'bubbles' elements up a list until a smaller value is reached.

Buffer: A small storage area used to store information on a temporary basis for compensating the difference in rates of flow of data between various computer devices. For example, when data flows from an I/O device to the CPU, it passes through a buffer.

Bug: An error in a computer programme. Although an hindrance, sometimes they are lucky accidents which open up new lines of approach to a problem.

Bugs: A problem that prevents a programme from working the way it is desired.

Built-in-functions: Sub-programmes, which are provided with the language so that the programmer need only to call them in a programme to have them automatically invoked. Also known as intrinsic sub-programmes.

Bullet: A symbol to indicate different lines.

Bundled: The inclusion of software with the hardware of a computer system as a part of the system's total price.

Burst: A set of packets transmitted back to back. Packet traffic tends to be bursty.

BUS: Internal communication path in a computer.

<body> html tag to indicate the content of a document.

<b> html tag to show the text in bold.

**
** html tag directing to begin a new line.

Bus: A means of exchanging information between the components of a computer.

Bus Topology: A network architecture in which all computers attach to a share medium, often a single cable. The bus architecture is mainly used for Local Area Networks.

Business to Business (B2B): Companies that seek business, not consumers, as customers.

Business to Consumer (B2C): Companies that market to consumers.

Button: Graphical representation of commands which has connections/linkages elsewhere e.g. button for undo will cancel implementation of the command last done.

Byte: A byte is made up of eight bits. It is a group of eight binary digits used to represent one unit of data in the computer's memory. The size of the computer's memory is measured in bytes. A megabyte is one million bytes.

Byte Stuffing: A protocol technique in which data is changed by inserting additional bytes to distinguish between data values and packet control values (i.e., headers).

C

C: A programming language, which was designed to have the virtues of high-level programming languages (mainly machine independence) with the efficiency of an assembly language.

C++: A programming language, which contains all the elements of the basic C language, but has been expanded to include numerous object-oriented programming features.

Cable Modem: A modem used to send digital information over the coaxial cables used for cable television.

Cache Memory: A small high speed memory, which is used to increase the speed of processing by making current programmes and data available to the CPU at a rapid rate.

CAI: Computer Assisted Instruction.

Calc: Spreadsheet software available in Open Office.

Call Statement: A programme statement, which transfers programme control to a subroutine.

Canonical Form: A Boolean function whose terms contain all variables (or their complements). This is the unreduced form of the Boolean function in minterm or maxterm form.

Capacitor: An electronic component which holds electricity for a certain period of time.

Capacity: The total number of data units (bits, nibbles, bytes, words) that a memory can store.

CAPS LOCK: A key used to shift alphabet characters from lower case to upper case.

Carrier: Any device, which is used to transmit data from one location to another.

Carrier Sense Multiple Access (CSMA): A network channel access method in which devices on the network send an intent-to-transmit message before actually sending data, to attempt to avoid a collision with other network transmissions.

Carrier Sense Multiple Access/Collision Detection (CSMA/CD): A version of CSMA in which network devices are able to sense a collision on the network and wait a random amount of time before retransmitting.

Carrier Signal: The basic signal transmitted across a network. A carrier is modulated (i.e., changed) to encode data.

Carry: The digit generated when the sum of two binary digits exceeds 1.

Carry Generation: The process of producing an output carry in a full-adder when both input bits are 1s.

Carry Propagation: The process of rippling an input carry to become the output carry in a full-adder when either or both of the input bits are 1s and the input carry is a 1.

Cascade: To connect "end-to-end" as when several counters are connected from the terminal count output of one counter to the enable input of the next counter.

Cascading: Connecting the output of one device to the input of a similar device, allowing one device to drive another in order to expand the operational capability.

Cassette Tape: A magnetic tape, similar to the those used on domestic taperecorders, designed for use in microcomputers.

CAT (Cable Address Translation): A form of NAT proposed by cable TV companies.

Category 5 Cable: A type of wiring needed for twisted pair Ethernet. The electrical characteristics of category 5 make it less susceptible to electrical interference than lower categories.

Cathode Ray Tube (CRT): An electronic tube with a TV like screen upon which information may be displayed.

CATV (Community Antenna TeleVision): The name applied to cable television systems. CATV technology uses frequency division multiplexing to propagate multiple television channels over a single cable simultaneously. See cable modem.

CAV (Constant Angular Velocity): Recording method used in magnetic disks (Winchester hard disks). In this method the angular velocity is same for all tracks. Thus tracks with smaller radius have a high linear velocity. The density of recording is higher in the innermost tracks.

C-band Transmission: The use of 4 GHz band of frequencies of transmission and retransmission of microwave signals in a satellite communication system.

CBR (Constant Bit Rate): The service used by ATM to transfer an audio or video stream. Data is sent at a steady rate.

CBT (Core Based Trees): A protocol for propagating multicast routing information.

CCITT: Stands Consultative Committee on International Telephone and Telegraph is the former name of the ITU.

CD: Compact disk or optical disk. These are flat circular secondary storage devices having large memory, e.g. 650 MB. Information is read with the help of laser which is coherent beam of light.

CD Drive: Acronym that stands for Compact Disk dive. It is a hardware component of the computer that houses and plays CDs.

CD-R: CD-recordable; an optical disk storage device on which data can be stored once.

CD-ROM: Short for compact disc-read-only memory. An optical disc (120cm in diameter and 1.5 mm thickness) which can store 700 and above megabytes of information.

CD-ROM Jukebox: A mass storage device, which uses a set of CD-ROM disks, disk drives, and a controller mounted in a single unit. All the CD-ROM disks of a CD-ROM jukebox form a single large storage unit. They are typically used for archiving read-only data.

CD-RW: CD-Rewritable; an optical disk storage on which data can be written and overwritten many times.

Cell: An area on a Karnaugh map the represents a unique combination of variables in product form; a single storage element in a memory; a fused cross point of a row and column in a PLD; a single storage element in a memory.

Cell Tax: A pejorative term used to refer to the 10 per cent header overhead introduced by ATM.

Central Processing Unit (CPU): The control unit and the arithmetic logic unit of a computer system are jointly known as the CPU. It is the brain of any computer system in which all calculations and comparisons performed by a computer are carried out. The CPU is also responsible for activating, and controlling operations of other units of a computer system.

CGI (Common Gateway Interface): A technology used to create dynamic World Wide Web documents. CGI programmes run on the server computer.

Chain Printer: A printer (to output results from a computer) in which the characters to be printed are embossed on a chain or a band. The chain is fashioned as a loop and print heads are activated to print specified characters.

Chain Printers: Line printers, which print characters by striking a set of hammers on a inked ribbon and paper placed against a metallic chain on which all the characters of the character set supported by the printer are embossed.

Channel: A small special purpose computer used to control the transfer of information between I/O units and the main memory of main frame computers.

Character: A single letter, numerical or special symbol, characters are represented by a number of bits.

Character Addressable Storage: A storage device, in which each character has one unique location with its own address. Another name for character addressable storage is variable-word-length storage.

Character Dialog Box: The dialog box for setting letter size, shape and colour.

Character Printer: A printer with a print mechanism, which prints one character at a time.

Charge-Coupled Device (CCD): A completely electronic storage device fabricated on semiconductor chips. It stores data as pocket of charge in a semi conductor.

Charles Babbage: The inventine genius of the 19th century who designed and made mechanical calculating machines. He is known as the father of computer.

Chat: An internet service that allows multiple users to communicate by entering text that is displayed on the screens of other participants.

Checksum: A value used to verify the data is not corrupted during transmission. The sender computes a checksum by adding the binary values of the data, and transmits the result in a packet with the data. A receiver computes a checksum over the data received, and compares the value to the checksum in the packet. See CRC.

Chip: A thin wafer of silicon on which integrated electronic components are deposited.

CIDR (Classless Inter-Domain Routing): The IP addressing and routing scheme that replaced classful addressing. CIDR uses a 32-bit address mask to denote the boundary between the prefix and suffix of an IP address.

Circle: Instruction in BASIC for drawing circle.

Circuit: A collection of electric or electronic components having wires or links between them. An integrated circuit has all these components and links on one silicon chip.

Circuit Switching: The simplest method of data communication in which a dedicated physical path is established between the sending and the receiving stations through the nodes of the network for the complete duration of information exchange.

CISC (Complex Instruction Set Computer): A processor which has variable length instructions, variety of addressing modes and many instructions.

CL (Connection Less): Characteristic of a network in which each transmission is independent. The alternative to connectionless networking is connection-oriented networking. See connection-oriented.

Classful Addressing: Characteristic of the original IP addressing scheme in which unicast addresseswere divided into three primary classes. The class of an address determines the division between the prefix and suffix in the address. See classes addressing.

Classless Addressing: Characteristic of the current IP addressing scheme in which a 32-bit address mask is used to determine the division between the prefix and suffix of an IP address. See classful addressing.

Classless Interdomain Routing (CIDR): A scheme for IP addressing that replaces the Class A, B, and C addressing system. CIDR allows for one IP address to be used designate additional unique IP addresses. A CIDR IP address looks like a standard IP address with a slash followed by a number appended to the end; for example: 206.224.65.194/12.

Clear: An asynchronous input used to reset a flip-flop (make the *Q* output 0); to place a register or counter in the state in which it contains all 0s.

Click: Press and release left mouse button once.

Click On: Perform an action by using mouse to select a button, menu or place cursor at specified location.

Client: When two programmes communicate over a network, a client is the one that initiates communication, while the programme that waits to be contacted is a server. A given programme can act as a server for one service and a client for another.

Client Computer: In a client-server computing environment, a computer, which is used by an end user to interact with the server computer. It runs client processes, which send service requests to the server.

Client Server Computing: A methodology of architecturing compute applications in which required functions are grouped as service requestors and service providers. Clients request services and servers provide them. This method is particularly suited for application implemented on distributed computers.

Client Server Network: A network where some programmes and files are stored in one computer can be shared by all computers. Each computer connected to the network can also run on its own.

Client-server Computing: A network of computers, which consists of a server computer (such as, file server, database server, print server, name server), and multiple client computers, which share programmes and data from the server.

Client-server Paradigm: The method of interaction used when two application programmes communicate over a network. A server application waits at a known address, and a client application contacts the server.

ClipArt: A programme having store of wide variety of readymade pre-drawn pictures, photographs, sounds and video clips that one can copy and insert in documents/worksheets or presentations.

Clip Art Library: A collection of graphic images stored on disk, which can be readily used in word processing or desktop publishing documents, or in presentation graphics, or for other purposes.

Clipboard: An invisible window holding copied or cut data e.g. for shifting picture from one location to another. When we cut/ copy it from original location, the picture gets attached to clipboard.

Clock: The basic timing signal in a digital system; a periodic waveform in which the interval between pulses equals the time for one bit.

Clock Speed: The number of times the built-in electronic clock of a computer system pulses in one second.

Close: To exit an activity or file or programme.

Cluster: A form of addressing used by Ipv6 in which a set of computers is assigned one address; a datagram sent to the address can be delivered to any one of the computers in the set. See broadcast, multicast, and unicast.

CLV (Constant Linear Velocity): Recording method used in CDROM in which the angular velocity of the disk is reduced as the recording head moves to the inner tracks. This maintains constant recording density on all the tracks of the disk.

CMOS: Complementary metal oxide semiconductor; a class of integrated logic circuits that is implemented with a type of field-effect transistor.

CMTS (Cast Modem Termination System): A technology used to control digital cable modems and allow a user to select content.

Co (Connection-Oriented): Characteristic of a network in which a connection must be established before data can be sent, and terminated after all data has been transferred. The alternative to connection-oriented networking. Note: the acronym CO is also used to refer to a telephone company Central Office. See connectionless.

Coaxial Cable: A type of cable used for computer networks as well as for cable television. The name arises from the structure in which a metal shield surrounds a center wire. The shield protects the signal on the inner wire from electrical interference.

COBOL: Common Business Oriented Language. A high level language used for business data processing.

Code: (1) The statements of a computer programme. (2) A set of rules outlining the way in which data may be represented (like BCD, EBCDIC, ASCII).

Code Generator: A very high-lever programming language in which programmers specify through an interactive dialog with the system, the design specifications of a system (which tasks are to be performed), and it automatically generates (produces) the programme source code for the system.

Coding: The process of writing computer instructions in a programming language.

Cog: A small, toothed wheel.

Cognitive Graphics: This deals with algorithms to recognize and classify pictures.

Cold Fusion: A dynamic Web page technology that allows items in a page to come from a conventional database. The sever interprets SQL queries embedded in each page whenever the page is requested.

Collage: A single picture formed by pasting parts of different pictures or objects.

Collate Sequence: An ordering assigned to the characters of a character set to be used for sequencing purposes. A commonly encountered collating sequence involves the special characters, letters, and digits, in that order.

Collector: One of the three regions in a bipolar transistor.

Collision: An event that occurs on a CSMA/CD network when two stations attempt to transmit simultaneously. The signals interfere with each other, forcing the two stations to back off and try again.

Colon Hexadecimal Notation: The syntactic notation used to express and IPv6 address.

.Com: A programme file extension.

Com: Computer output microform or to microfilm.

Combination Circuit: A group of logic gates interconnected to form a logic circuit.

Combination Mode: The mode of an OLMC in which a combination logic function is implemented.

Combinational Logic: A combination of logic gates interconnected to produce a specified Boolean function with no storage or memory capability; sometimes called combinatorial logic.

Command: Portion of an instruction which specifies the operation to be performed.

Command Interpreter: The part of an operating system, which serves as an interface for the user to communicate with the computer via its operating system.

Command-line Interface: A textual user interface in which the user gives instructions to the computer by typing commands using the keyboard.

Comment: An entry in a computer programme for the purpose of documentation or explanation. Comments are used within a programme to assist anyone reading the source programme listing. They do not contain any programme logic, and are ignored (not translated) by the language processor.

Common Business Oriented Language (COBOL): A high-level programming language developed for business data processing applications.

Common Carriers: Data transmission service providers.

Common Gateway Interface (CGI) Script: A simple programme that runs on the Net; guest books, for instance, often are CGI scripts.

Communication: Transfer of information between a transmitter and a receiver.

Communication Channel: A medium through which (electrical) signals are transmitted and received.

Communication Protocol: A set of rules and procedures established to interconnect and communicate between computers. It provides a method for orderly and efficient exchange of data by establishing rules for the proper interpretation of controls and data transmitted as raw bits and bytes.

Communications Satellite: A microwave relay station precisely positioned 36000 kms. above the equator with an orbit speed that exactly matches the earth's rotation speed. It is used for data transmission between any two randomly chosen points in very-very large area.

Commutative Law: In addition (ORing) and multiplication (ANDing) of two variables, the order in which the variables are ORed or ANDed makes no difference.

Compact Disk-Read-Only Memory (CD-ROM): A shiny, silver colour metal disk of 5¼ -inch (12 cm) diameter having a storage capacity of about 650 Megabytes. It is so called, because of its enormous storage capacity on a compact-size disk, and because it is a read-only storage medium.

Comparator: A digital circuit that compares the magnitudes of two quantities and produces an output indicating the relationship of the quantities.

Compile: To translate a programme written in a high-level language into its equivalent machine language programme. Usually a single source statement yields more than one machine instruction.

Complement: For a number, which has a n digits in it, a complement is defined as the difference between the number and the base raised to the nth power minus one. For example, complement of $37_{10} = 10^2 - 1 - 37 = 62^{10}$. In Boolean algebra, the complement of a variable is the reverse (NOT) of its value. For example, complement of A is $\bar{A}$.

Completely Connected Network: A network in which there is a separate physical link for connecting each node to any other node in the network.

Complex Instruction Set Computer (CISC) Architecture: An architecture of CPUs with large instruction set, variable-length instructions, and a variety of addressing modes.

Compliment: The inverse or opposite of a number, in Boolean algebra, the inverse function, expressed with the bar over the variable. The complement of a 1 is a 0 and vice versa.

Compression: Method of keeping the files in a computer at a reduced size (also called as Zipping).

Compute Aided Instruction (CAI): A self-learning course, using the computer.

Computer: An electronic device, which an automatically accept and store input data, process them, and produce output results by interpreting and executing programmed instructions.

Computer Aided Design (CAD): Use of computers to automate design and drafting operations.

Computer Aided Manufacturing (CAM): Use of computers to automate manufacturing operations.

Computer Animation: The area of computer science, which deals with the generation, sequencing, and display (at a specified rate) of a set of images (called frames) to create an effect of visual change or motion, similar to a movie film (video). Animation is commonly used those instances where videography is not possible, or animation can better illustrate the concept than video.

Computer Audio: The area of computer science, which deals with synthesizing, recording, and playback of audio or sound with the aid of a computer.

Computer Graphics: The area of computer science, which deals with the generation, representation, manipulation and display of pictures (line drawings and images) with the aid of a computer.

Computer Language: A set of rules or conventions for instructing the computer. BASIC, COBOL and JAVA are some of the computer languages.

Computer Literacy: Having sufficient computer knowledge, so that an individual can work and live in a computerized society.

Computer Network: A group of geographically distributed computers which are interconnected using communication lines in such a way that any computer in the group may be accessed or used from any other computer in the group.

Computer Programme: An organized code of commands for a specific purpose by a computer.

Computer System: Is a central processor together with its associated peripheral equipment. It is the complete assembly, hardware and software, with CPU, memory, input and output (I/O) devices, plus any other device for an intended application.

Computer System: The various components (input and output devices, storage, CPU) of a computer integrated together to perform the steps called for in the programme being executed.

Computer Video: The area of computer science, which deals with the recording and display of a sequence of images at a reasonable speed to create an impression of movement.

Computer-Aided Learning (CAL): Learning by using a computer.

Computer-Based Training (CBT): Using computer technologies for training and education. The use of computers helps in making tutoring programmes, which are tailored to the student's level of subject mastery, and can provide immediate feedback.

Concalenation: The process of combination strings.

Conditional Statement: The statements of a programme which are valid only in certain situations.

Conductor: Something which conducts electricity.

COnference on Data Systems Language (CODASYL): A committee of computer users, manufactures, and the United States Government, which helps to establish programming standards for various programming languages.

Congestion: A condition in which each packet sent through a network experiences excessive delay because the network is overrun with packets. Unless protocol software detects congestion and reduces the rate at which packets are sent, a network can experience congestion collapse.

Connectionless: A characteristic of a network system that allows a computer to send data to any other computer at any time. Connectionless networks are analogous to a postal system in which each letter carries the address of the recipient; letters can be sent at any time. See connection-oriented.

Connection-Oriented: Characteristic of a network in which a connection must be established before data can be sent, and terminated after all data has been transferred. The alternative to connection-oriented networking is connectionless networking. See connectionless.

Console: In a mainframe system, the terminal, which is directly connected to the host (main computer), and is mainly used by the system administrators to monitor the health of the system, or to perform some system administration activities.

Constant: A value, written into a programme instruction, which does not change during the execution of the programme.

Control Bus: A set of wires used to transmit signals to control the operation of various units of a computer.

Control Instruction Register (CIR): A special register (i.e., temporary storage location) which holds machine instructions. Currently being interpreted by the control unit.

Control Programme: An operating system programme, which controls the operations and management of resources of a computer system. The control programme's major functions are job scheduling, input/output scheduling, and programme monitoring.

Control Statements: Programme statements which enable to control the execution of a programme.

Control Unit: The unit of a computer system, which manages and coordinates the operations of all the other components of the computer system. It is one of the components of the central processing unit (CPU) of the computer.

Cookie: A small value a Web server passes to a browser in a reply to help the server identify the user. A browser returns the cookie when sending subsequent requests from the user to the server that issued the cookie.

Copy: To reproduce data in a new location or other destination, leaving the source data unchanged.

Copy Right: Right of a person or institution on original creations, pictures, video clipping and software. Copyright prevent others from using these material without permission of the copyright holder.

Coral: A programming language for military applications.

CORBA (Common Object Request Broker Architecture): An object-oriented middleware technology.

Core Storage/Memory: A high speed memory which is internal to the computer.

Corel DRAW: An application software for vector drawing.

Counter: A device, register or storage location for storing integers, which is suitably incremented or decremented to represent the number of occurrences of an event.

CPLD: Complex programmable logic device.

CPU: Is an abbreviation for Central Processing Unit. It is the computer module in-charge of fetching, decoding and executing instructions. It contains a control unit, an ALU and other related facilities.

CPU Scheduler: The part of an operating system, which is concerned with deciding which of the ready jobs should be allotted the CPU for execution.

CPU-bound Jobs: Jobs which heavily utilize the CPU operations during the course of their processing.

Crash: A hardware or software failure that causes a computer system to stop functioning.

CRC (Cyclic Redundancy Check): A value used to verify that data is not corrupted during transmission. The sender computes a CRC and transmits the result in a packet with the data. A receiver computes the CRC over the data received, and compares the value to the CRC in the packet. A CRC is more complex to compute than a checksum, but can detect more transmission errors.

Credit Card: A small plastic card which is used instead of cash to pay for things.

Cross Translator: A programme to translate a high level language to the machine language of some machine *X* and run on another machine *Y*.

CRT: Cathod Ray Tube; a visual display unit having a television like screen.

Cryptography: A means of protecting private information against unauthorized access in those situations where it is difficult to ensure access control. The basic idea behind this security technique is that, if it is not possible to ensure access control, it is better to prevent comprehension of information.

CSMA (Carrier Sense Multiple Access): The technique used with bus architecture networks in which computers attached to the common bus check for the presence of a carrier before transmitting.

CSMA/CD (Carrier Sense Multiple Access with Collision Detection): A CSMA network that has the capability to detect errors that result when multiple stations transmit simultaneously. See collision.

CUPL: Compiler for Universal Programmable Logic; a software compiler language for PLD programming; a type of hardware description language.

Current Sinking: The action of a circuit in which it accepts current into its output from a load.

Current Sourcing: The action of a circuit in which it sends current out of its output and into a load.

Cursor: A highlight on the screen of a monitor, which indicates the location of the next keyed-in character on the display screen. It can appear as a small rectangular object, line, arrow, or I-beam pointer, or in a spreadsheet, as a large block covering an entire cell.

Cut: Removing a file or part of a file for fixing else where.

Cut: Removing a file or part of a file for pasting else where.

Cybernatics: The use of computers coupled with automatic machinery to carry out complex operations.

Cybernetics: The mathematical science of the transmission and transformation of measurable information.

Cyberspace: The world-wide network of computers.

Cycle Stealing: The method used to transfer data from I/O units to memory by suspending the memory – CPU data transfer for one memory cycle.

Cycle Time: The time interval between the instant at which a read/ write command is given to a memory, and the instant when the next such instruction can be issued to the memory (also known as memory cycle time).

Cylinder: In a disk pack, a set of corresponding tracks on all the surfaces is called a cylinder. All tracks of a cylinder are accessible by a single movement of access mechanism.

D

D Channel: The term telephone companies use to denote a channel configured to handle data. ISDN includes D channel service. See B channel.

D Flip-flop: A type of bistable multivibrator in which the output assumes the state of the D input on the triggering edge of a clock pulse.

Daisy Wheel Printer: A letter-quality printer, which uses a printing head with the appearance of daisy and/or a wheel. Each petal of the daisy wheel has a character embossed on it.

DASD: Acronym for Direct-Access Storage Device; for such devices time required to retrieve data is independent of the physical location of the data.

DAT (Digital Audio Tape): Uses 4 mm wide magnetic tape in a cartridge to back up contents of disk.

Data: Denotes any or all facts, numbers, letters and symbols that refer to or describe an object, idea, condition, situation or other factors suitable for communication, interpretation or processing by people or by automatic means.

Data Base Management System (DBMS): A set of programmes provided to facilitate the users in organizing, crating, deleting, updating, and manipulating their data in a database.

Data Bus: A bidirectional set of conductive paths on which data or instruction codes are transferred into the microprocessor or on which the result of an operation or computation is sent out from the microprocessor.

Data Capture: Data collection performed in the course of a transaction.

Data Definition Language (DDL): A language used to define the structure of a data base.

Data Dependence: Dependency of data on the application.

Data Dictionary: A document, which maintains the data definitions of a database. It is automatically crated/updated by the DDL as the data base schema is defined or changed.

Data Element: A meaningful collection of related characters. Also called a field or data item.

Data Entry: The conversion of human readable data into a form, which a computer system can interpret. This is also called data preparation.

Data Entry Unit: A system with a keyboard to enter data and a magnetic medium such as a floppy disk to store the entered data.

Data File: A collection of related records.

Data Integrity: Consistency of data in all files.

Data Manipulation Language (DML): A language used to enter and manipulate the data in a database.

Data Processing: Acquiring and transforming the data into a useful form.

Data Processing System: A system that accomplishes data processing. It includes the necessary resources, which are people, procedures and devices needed to process the data.

Data Redundancy: Repetition of the same data items in more than one file.

Data Selector: A circuit that selects data from several inputs one at a time in a sequence and places them on the output; also called a multiplexer.

Data Sheet: A document that specifies parameter values and operating conditions for an integrated circuit or other device.

Data Storage Hierarchy: In data processing organization of data into growing hierarchy for easy manageability. A typical data storage hierarchy consists of bits, characters, fields, records, files and database.

Data Transfer Rate: The speed at which data is transferred from main memory to another medium on which data are recorded. For magnetic tape, the data transfer rate is equal to the product of the tape speed and recording density. In a network environment, it refers to the speed of transfer of data from one computer to another on the network.

Database: A collection of data files integrated and organized into a single comprehensive file system, which is arranged to minimize duplication of data, and to provide convenient access to information within that system to satisfy a wide variety of user needs.

Database Administrator: One who is responsible for defining, updating, and controlling access to a data base.

Database Model: The manner in which the various files of a database are linked together. The four commonly used database models are hierarchical, network, relational and object-oriented.

Database Schema: The database structure definition.

Database Software: A set of programmes, which enables users to create a database, maintain it (add, delete and update its records), organize its data in desired fashion, and to selectively retrieve useful information from it.

Data-link Layer: Layer 2 of the OSI model, the Data-Link layer packages data from the upper layers into frames and then transmits them onto the media. To do this, it must define a set of rules for flow-and-error control and assign physical addresses to each device on the link. To this end, layer 2 is commonly split into two sublayers: Logical Link Control (LLC) and Media Access Control (MAC).

DATE (Data Terminal Equipment): A telephone company term for equipment such as a computer that connects to a network. See DCE.

DB Connector: A type of physical connector used with computers and communication equipment. The number immediately following the dash specifies the number of pins. For example, DB-9, DB-15, and DB-25 connectors have 9, 15, and 25 pins.

DBMS (Database Management System): Programmes for forming, accessing and maintaining a database.

DCE (Data Communication Equipment): A telephone company term for communication equipment such as a modem. See DTE. Note: the acronym is also used for Distributed Computing Environment.

DDR (Double Data Rate): A mechanism used to produce computer memory.

De Compression: Process of enlarging a compressed file in a computer to its original size (Also called unzipping).

De Morgan's Theorem: A theorem in Boolean algebra, which stats how to complement a Boolean expression.

Debug: Checking the logic and design of a programme to locate and eliminate errors.

Debugger: A software tool, which helps the programmer in debugging the logic of a programme by allowing him/her to follow the programme's execution step-by-step, and to display intermediate calculation results and field values whenever desired.

Debugging: The process of eliminating problems (bugs) in a programme.

Decade: Characterized by ten states or values.

Decade Counter: A digital counter having ten states.

Decimal: Describes a number system with a base of ten.

Decimal Number System: A number system with a base of 10. The ten allowable digits are 0, 1, 2, 3, 4, 5, 6, 7, 8, and 9. It is used in our day-to-day life.

Decision Logic: A selection logic.

Decode: A stage of the DSP pipeline operation in which instructions are assigned to functional units and are decoded.

Decoder: The part of CPU, which has the necessary circuitry to decode and interpret the meaning of every instruction supported by the CPU.

Decrement: To decrease the binary state of a counter by one.

Dedicated Line: See leased line.

Default: A standard setting by software or hardware till the user does not change it.

Default Route: A wild-card entry in a routing table. The routing software follows the default route if the table does not contain an explicit route to the destination.

Delay-bandwidth Product: A measure of a network that specifies the amount of data that is present in the network between the sender and receiver.

Delete: This command shifts a file/folder to the recycle bin or deletes the selected portion.

Delete Key: Key that deletes a character or selected text or graphics.

Demand Paging: A procedure used to bring from the disk memory to the main memory of a computer the portion of a programme (a page) to be executed.

Demarc: A telephone company term for the boundary between communication facilities owned by the telephone company and facilities owned by a private organization See NIU and NTI.

Demodulator: A device that accepts a modulated carrier wave and extracts the information used to modulate it. See modem.

Demultipelxer (DEMUX): A circuit (digital device) that switches digital data from one input line to several output lines in a specified time sequence.

Demultiplex: A general concept that refers to separating information received over a common communication channel into its original components. Demultiplexing occurs both in hardware (i.e., electrical signals can be demultiplexed) and in software (i.e., protocol software can demultiplex incoming messages and pass each to the correct application programme). See multiplex.

Denial-of-service Attack: See DOS.

Dependency Notation: A notational system for logic symbols that specifies input and output relationships, thus fully defining a given function; an integral part of ANSI/IEEE Std. 91-1984.

Design Phase: A phase in the life-cycle of software system during which the detailed design of the system selected in the study phase occurs.

Desktop: The background of the screen on which windows icons and dialog boxes appear.

Desktop Publishing (DTP): An application software package, which allows a user to perform design, typesetting, and paste-up functions, and to product high-quality, camera-ready printed pages of the documents so prepared on a high-quality printer.

Desk-top System: A computer that fits completely on an office desk.

Destination Address: An address in a packet that specifies the ultimate destination to which the packet is sent. In a hardware frame, the destination address must be a hardware address. In an IP datagram, the destination address must be an IP address.

Development Phase: A phase in the life-cycle of a software system during which a system is constructed to meet the requirements specified in the design phase.

Device Driver: A programme that must be installed to run an attached device of a computer.

DHCP (Dynamic Host Configuration Protocol): A protocol that computers use to obtain configuration information. DHCP allows a computer to be assigned an IP address without requiring a manager to configure information about the computer in a server's database.

Diagnostic Routines: Programmes used to print error messages by a computer to indicate system problems, and improper programme instructions.

Dialect: A particular version of a programming language which is different from other versions (dialects) of the same language.

Dialog Box: A window that appear on the screen when we work on a computer asking next path of work or directing certain actions.

Dial-up Line: A data transmission service, which operates in a manner similar to a telephone call. Also known as switched line.

Dialup Modem: A modem uses the dialup telephone network to communicate. Dialup modems use an audible tone as a carrier wave, and must be able to dial or answer a telephone call.

Difference: The result of a subtraction.

Digit: A symbol used to express a quantity.

Digital: Having a discrete set of values, as opposed to a continuous set of values (See ANALOG).

Digital Camera: A camera which uses digital technology to capture images, instead of a photographic film. The digital image is stored in the memory of camera and this can be transferred to an outside storage device like hard disk.

Digital Channel:A communication medium through which information in binary (digital) form is transmitted.

Digital Computer: A computer, which works with discrete quantities. It uses numbers to simulate real-time processes. Compare with analog computer.

Digital Signal Processor: A microprocessor which is optimized to process real-time audio and video signals.

Digital Signature: Data encrypted in such a way that the receiver can verify the identity of the sender.

Digitizer: An input device used for converting (digitizing) pictures, maps and drawings into digital form for storage in computers. This enables re-creation of the drawing from the stores information when required, and easy incorporation of changes in the drawing as and when required.

Dijkstra's Algorithm: An algorithm for computing shortest paths in a graph Routing protocols use Dijkstra's algorithm to compute optimal routes.

Dim: Command in BASIC to show the maximum number of members in an array.

DIMM: Dual in-line memory module.

Diode: A semi-conductor device that conducts current in only one direction.

DIP: Dual in-line package; a type of IC package whose leads must pass through holes to the other side of a PC board.

Direct Access: Getting an item of information directly from a file in a storage device.

Direct Address: The address of an operand in main memory specified in an instruction.

Direct File: A file organization in which the desired record (piece of information) can be directly located by its key field value without having to search through a sequence of other records. Also known as random file.

Direct/leased-line Connection: A method of connecting a computer to the internet by using a dedicated (leased) telephone line.

Directed Broadcast: A broadcast to all computers on a remote network achieved by sending a single copy of the packet to the remote network and broadcasting the packet when it arrives. TCP/IP supports directed broadcast.

Directory: A mapping table, which is used by operating systems to map file names to their corresponding file attributes and file data, and also to provide greater flexibility to users in file naming.

Disk: A form of backing storage. A magnetic disk on which data or programmes may be stored and referred to as and when required. Also spelt as Disc.

Disk Array: A mass storage device, which uses a set of hard disks, hard disk drives, and a controller mounted in a single box. All the disks of a disk array form a single large storage unit. Also known as Redundant Array or Inexpensive Disks (RAID).

Disk Drive: A device the holds a floppy disk or a hard disk and reads and writes data using a read/write head.

Disk Memory: A secondary or peripheral memory in which information is stored as magnetized spots on the surface of disks coated with magnetic material. In hard disks the disks are not flexible. In floppy disks the disk is a circular platter made of flexible magnetic coated plastic sheet.

Disk Pack: A removable direct-access storage medium cont-aining multiple magnetic disks mounted vertically on a single shaft.

Diskette: A low-cost, thin and flexible magnetic storage device used on small computer systems. Also called a floppy disk.

Display Card: A electronic circuit card used to transfer information from CPU to monitor.

Display File: A file containing a sequence of instructions (programme) to draw a picture on a graphic output unit.

Distance-vector: An algorithm that routers use to compute optimal routes to each destination. Periodically, each router receives routing information from neighbouring routers. A router replaces a current route if a lower cost route become available. See link-status and SPF.

Distributed Computers: A configuration in which several workstations or PCs are interconnected by a fast communication network.

Distributed Computing System: A computer system consisting of interconnected multiple computers.

Distributed Database: Seamless integration of multiple databases located on different computers. A distributed database management system functions in a manner that the multiple distributed databases managed by it appear as a single and centralized database to the end users.

Distributed Spanning Tree: An algorithm that bridges use when they boot to detect and break cycles.

Distributive Law: The law that states that ORing several variables and then ANDing the result with a single variable is equivalent to ANDing the single variable with each of the several variables and then ORing the product.

Dividend: In a division operation, the quantity that is being divided.

Divisior: In a division operation, the quantity that is divided into the dividend.

DIX Ethernet (Digital Intel Xerox Ethernet): A term used for the original Ethernet because the standard was developed jointly by the three companies.

DLT: Digital linear tape; a type of magnetic tape format.

DMA: Direct memory access. This is a method in which data from I/O devices to memory and vice-versa is transmitted without the involvement of the central processing unit of a computer.

DNS (Domain Name System): The automated system used to translate computer names into equivalent IP addresses. A DNS server responds to a query by looking up the name and returning the address. See domain.

DOCSIS (Data Over Cable System Interface Standard): A standard for sending digital information over a cable modem system.

Document: Collection of information or texts prepared for to use in a software.

Document Area/Client Area: Area in window for preparing text or image.

Documentation: Documentation of a software system involves collecting, organizing, storing and maintaining a complete historical record of programmes and other documents used or prepared during the different phases of the systems.

Domain: Domain is what comes before the "com" or "net" or "edu," all of which are known as top-level domains; for example, McGarvey.net is the name of the author's Internet domain.

Domain Name: Unique name of server computer system which handles Web Pages, delivery and receipt of e-mails, etc. The part of an e-mail address after @ is domain name of the site, e.g. in crc@**giasdl01.vsnl.net.in** the portion with bold letters is domain name.

Domain Name Service (DNS): A translation service that correlates domain names into IP addresses.

"Don't care": A combination of input literals that cannot occur and are used as 1s or 0s on a Karnaugh map.

Dos: Disk-based operating system.

DOS (Denial of Service): A form of network attack in which a site is flooded with so many packets (usually incorrect or fictitious requests) that the site cannot respond to legitimate requests.

Dot Matrix Printer: A printing device which prints characters as a pattern of closely-spaced dots produced by a set of tiny pins.

Dots Per Inch (DPI): A measurement of quality of the printed output. It refers to the number of dots which can be printed per linear inch horizontally or vertically.

Dotted Decimal Notation: The syntactic notion used to express a 32-bit IPv4 address. Each octet is written in decimal with a period separating octets.

Double Click: Two quick clicks on a mouse button without moving the mouse. Used for starting a programme or programme features shown through icons.

Downlink: The path of data transmitted from a satellite to an earth station. See uplink.

Download: To transfer a file from one computer system to another. One can download a programme from the Internet.

Downloading: Moving a file from a remote computer to one's own computer in a network environment.

Downstream: The path of data from the Internet to a residential customer. The term is often used with DSL or cable modem technologies. See upstream.

Downtime: The period during which a computer is malfunctioning or not operating correctly due to machine failures.

Dpi-Dots Per Inch: The unit of resolution indicating the number of dots printed per inch of a raster picture.

DPU: Display processing unit consists of a set of electronic logic circuits to generate signals to drive a display device using the programme in the display file. It also accepts inputs from graphic input device(s) to store and interactively manipulate displayed pictures.

Drag: Pressing the mouse button, holding it and then moving the mouse. An image or block of text can be moved by dragging.

Drag and Drop: Holding down the left mouse button and moving the mouse until a desired location is reached, and then releasing the left mouse button to drop the item.

Drain: One of the terminal of a field-effect transistor.

DRAM: Dynamic random-access memory; a type of semiconductor memory that uses capacitors as the storage elements and is a volatile, read/write memory.

Drum Printers: Line printers, which print characters by striking a set of hammers on an inked ribbon and paper placed against a solid cylindrical drum with characters embossed on its surface in the form of circular bands.

DS-0, DS-1, DS-3 (Digital Signal Level Standards): The designations that telephone companies use for the speeds of popular point-to-point digital circuits. DS-0 denotes a digital voice circuit of 64 Kbps; DS-1 denotes 1.5444 Mbps; and DS-3 denotes 44.736 Mbps. See T1, T3.

DSL (Digital Subscribe Line): A generic reference to any of the services such as ADSL and HDSL that supply broadband data rates over telephone lines.

DST (Distributed Spanning Tree): The algorithm bridges use to avoid a loop.

DSU/CSU (Data Service Unit/Channel Service Unit): An electronic device that connects a leased digital data circuit to computer equipment. The DSU/CSU translates between the digital format used by the telephone companies and the format used by the computer industry. See modem.

DTMF (Dual Tone Multi-Frequency): The touch tone encoding used with telephones.

DTP (Desk Top Publishing): Desktop Publishing. Using personal computer and graphics software to design, and print pages complete with pictures and text.

Dumb Terminal: A terminal that can function only when linked to a computer.

Dump Variable: A variable used to store temporarily the contents of another variable in order to avoid loss of data.

Duplex: A link that allows simultaneous two-way communication.

Duty Cycle: The ratio of pulse width to period expressed as a percentage.

DV (Distance Vector): One of two basic algorithms used by routing protocols. The alternative to distance vector routing is link-status routing.

DVDROM: Digital Video Disk Read Only Memory used a technology for storing data on a disk similar to CDROM except that 2 to 4 layers are used to record information. Data is also packed on the tracks much closer compared to CDROM. The maximum capacity of 4 layer DVDROM is 17 GB. Rewritable versions are also emerging.

DVMRP (Distance Vector Multicast Routing Protocol): The multicast routing protocol used on the MBONE, DVMRP sends multicast locally, but uses IP-in-IP tunneling to transfer multicast datagrams among sites.

DWDM (Dense Wavelength Division Multiplexing): A high-speed multiplexing technology used with optical fiber.

Dynamic Data Exchange (DDE): A technique for linking applications, which allows a user to move data from one application another, such as from a spreadsheet into a word-processor. Changes made in one application are automatically reflected in linked applications.

Dynamic Document: A computer programme, associated with a World Wide Web document, that can generate a document on demand. When a browser requests a dynamic document, the server runs the programme and sends the output to the browser. A dynamic document programme can generate different output for each request. See active document, static document, and URL.

Dynamic Host Configuration Protocol (DHCP): A part of the TCP/IP protocol suite, DHCP dynamically assigns IP addresses to network devices.

Dynamic Memory: A type of semiconductor memory having capacitive storage cells that lose stored data over a period of time and, therefore, must be refreshed.

Dynamic RAM (DRAM): A type of RAM, which uses an external circuitry to periodically "regenerate" or refresh the storage charge to retain the stored data.

E

E^2CMOS: Electrically erasable CMOS (EECMOS); the circuit technology used for the reprogrammable cells in a GAL.

EBCDIC (Extended Binary Coded Decimal Interchange Code): A standard that assigns unique values to 256 characters, including upper and lower case letters, digits, punctuation, and control characters. See ASCII.

Echo Reply: A message used for testing and debugging. An ICMP echo reply is returned in answer to an ICMP echo request message. The ping programme receives echo replies. See echo request.

Echo Request: A message use for testing and debugging. The ping programme sends ICMP echo request messages to elicit echo replies. See echo reply.

ECL: Emitter-coupled logic; a class of integrated logic circuit that are implemented with nonsaturating bipolar junction transistors.

Ede-trigged Flip-flop: Any type of flip-flop in which the data are entered and appear on the output on the same clock edge.

Edit: To modify the form or format of the data by inserting or deleting characters where needed.

Edit Menu: Menu showing options for editing text and pictures (cut, copy, paste etc.).

Editor: A system programme which performs the operations mentioned under edit.

EDO DRAM: Extended data output dynamic random-access memory.

EDP: Acrynym for Electronic Data Processing.

Education Software: Software, which allows computer systems to be used as a teaching and learning tool.

EEPROM: Electrically Erasable Programmable Read Only Memory in which information may be erased and written using electrical signals.

Effective Address: The address in main memory, calculated by the CPU, which is used to retrieve operands.

EGP (Exterior Gateway Protocol): Term applied to any route propagation protocol used to transfer routing information among Autonomous Systems. See IGP.

Electrically EPROM (EEPROM): An EPROM chip in which the stored information is erased by using high voltage electric pulses. Also known as flash memory.

Electronic: A term used to refer to equipment which uses components like transistors and valves to control the current.

Electronic Card: A small plastic card having encoded data appropriate for the application for which it is used. An electronic-card reader, which is normally connected to a computer, is used to read the data encoded on an electronic card and transfer it to the computer for further processing.

Electronic Cottage: Because of the computers, human beings will not have to move out of their homes as every information and facility would be available at home itself, even one's job. Such a condition would mean an electronic cottage.

Electronic Data Interchange (EDI): The use of computers and data communications to transmit data electronically between computers.

Electronic Funds Transfer (EFT): A general term referring to a cashless approach used to pay for goods and services. Electronic signals between computers are often used to adjust the accounts of the parties involved in a transaction.

Electronic Mail: Facility for sending the text of a document by data transmission particularly it is kept in store at the receiving end for retrieval when required, rather than being delivered in a printed form.

Electronic Pen: An input device, which serves as an effective point-and-draw device.

Electrothermal Printer: A high-speed printer, which uses heated elements to create characters as matrices of small dots on heat-sensitive paper.

Elementary Data Item: A data item, which is not broken down into smaller units.

Else IF: Command in BASIC, applied when the condition following IF is not satisfied.

E-mail (Electronic Mail): Abbreviation for electronic mail. Takes a message from one computer to another computer any where on globe.

Emitter: One of the three regions in a bipolar junction transistor.

Emulation: Technique allowing one computer to run programmes written for another of different design.

Emulator: A programme, which permits one computer to execute the machine-language instructions of another computer of different make.

Enable: To activate or put into an operational mode; an input on a logic circuit that enables its operation.

Encapsulation: The technique in which information to be sent is placed inside the data area of a packet or frame. A packet from one protocol can be encapsulated in another (e.g., ICMP can be encapsulated in IP).

Encoder: A digital circuit (device) that converts information to a coded form.

Encryption: The process of transforming an intelligible information into an unintelligible form.

Encryption Key: The short value used when encrypting data to guarantee confidentiality. In some encryption schemes, the receiver must use the same key to decrypt the data. Other schemes use a pair of keys—one to encrypt and a different key to decrypt.

End: Instruction in BASIC to show that the programme is over.

End Key: The key which moves the cursor to the 'end' position defined by the application programme.

End User: Any individual who uses the information generated by a computer based system.

Endpoint Address: A generic term for any address assigned to a computer that can be used as a destination address. For example, an IP address is one type of endpoint address.

End-to-end: Characteristic of any protocol or function that operates on the original source and ultimate destination, but not on intermediate computers (e.g., not on routers).

End-to-end Solution: A computerized solution offered to a user in which a single vendor takes the responsibility of supplying all the hardware and software components of the solution.

End-to-tape (EOT) Marker: A reflective marker, which indicates the end of the usable tape.

Enter: Inputing data into the computer through the key board.

Enter Key: The key, when pressed, transmits instruction to the computers. When it is pressed the cursor will move to the beginning of the next line.

Entertainment Software: Software, which allows computer system to be used as an entertainment tool.

EPROM (Erasable Programmable Read Only Memory): Erasable Programmable Read Only Memory. A semiconductor memory where programmes are semi-permanently stored. The programme may be erased and new information written in it.

Erase: Erasing data from floppy disc or hard disc.

Error: A mistake causing a computer programme to produce incorrect results.

Error Detection: The process of detecting bit errors in a digital code.

Error Message: A display on screen showing error in programme execution or input.

Esc Button: Left top button on a keyboard.

Ethernet: A popular Local Area Network technology that uses a shared bus topology and CSMA/CD access. Basic Ethernet operates at 10 Mbps, Fast Ethernet operates at 100 Mbps, and Gigabit Ethernet operates at 1000 Mbps (i.e., 1 Gbps).

10/100 Ethernet: An Ethernet interface that can automatically sense the maximum speed of a connected device and choose to operate at 10 Mbps or 100 Mbps.

Even Parity: A parity bit added to a unit of data, usually each character, to make the number of *1* bits even. A receiver checks the parity to determine whether data has been corrupted during transmission. See odd parity.

Exclusive–OR (XOR): A basic logic operation in which a HIGH occurs when the two inputs are at opposite levels.

Exclusive-NOR (XNOR) Gate: A logic gate that produces a LOW only when the two inputs are at opposite levels.

Exclusive-OR (XOR) Gate: A logic gate that produces a HIGH only when the two inputs are at opposite levels.

Execution Time: The total time required to execute a programme on a particular system is called its execution time for that computer system.

Executive Programme: A system programme used to monitor I/O devices and to allocate computer resources to user programmes.

Exit: To stop the operation of a programme and switch back to the operating system of the computer.

Explicitly Parallel Instruction Computing (EPIC): A technology, which is fast emerging as the technology for next-generation processors. The three key features used in this technology for improved processor performance are explicit parallelism, predication and speculation.

Exponent: The part of a floating point number that represents the number of places that the decimal point (or binary point) is to be moved.

Extended Binary Coded Decimal Interchange Code (EBCDIC): An 8-bit coding system, developed by IBM, which is used to represent characters in many computer.

Extension: The identification part of the files name that comes after the dot (.) symbol.

Extension Header: An optional header used in the IPv6 protocol.

Exterior Switch: A switch in a packet switched network to which host computers connect. See interior switch.

Extranet: An internet connection between a predetermined number of member organizations.

Eye of Gnome: The GNU/Linux software to view pictures.

F

F: It is a block of information. It can be lines of text, document, data, graphics, worksheet, programme, etc.

Facsimile (FAX): Transmission of pictures, texts, maps, graphs, etc., over transmission lines, phone lines, and other carriers between geographically separated points. An image is scanned at a transmitting point, and duplicated at a receiving point.

Fall Time: The time interval between the 90 per cent point and the 10 per cent point on the negative-going edge of a pulse.

Fame Type: One of four standards that defines the structure of an Ethernet packet: Ethernet 802.3, Ethernet 802.2, Ethernet SNAP or Ethernet II. Most networks can identify the frame type automatically.

Fan-out: The number of equivalent gate inputs of the same family series that a logic gate can drive.

Fascimile: An exact copy.

Fast Ethernet: A version of Ethernet technology that operates at 100 Mbps.

Fax Facsimile: This deals with the electronic transmission of a document from one point to another.

FDD Connector: Cable that connects Floppy Disk Driver with motherboard.

FDDI (Fibre Distributed Data Interface): It is a standard defined by ISO/ANSI and IEEE for local area network using Fibre Optic cables to interconnect workstations/computers.

FDM (Frequency Division Multiplexing): Characteristic of a mechanism used to share a communication medium among multiple senders in which each sender is assigned a unique frequency or channel. Because they use separate frequencies, the simultaneous transmissions do not interfere with one another. See TDM.

Feasibility Study: A study to determine whether the proposed solution is technically and economically feasible in all respect.

Feeder Circuit: A term used with cable television that refers to the wiring between a neighbourhood concentration point and individual subscribers. A feeder circuit is less than two miles long. See trunk circuit.

FET: Field-effect transistor.

Fetch : An operation involving going to the memory and getting an instruction and then decoding it in the control unit.

Fiber: Abbreviation for optical fiber.

Fiber Modem: A modem that uses modulated light waves to provide digital communication. A fiber modem uses light emitting diodes or lasers to transmit light. See optical fiber.

Fibre Optics Cable: A cable made of glass fibres used to transmit light signals.

Field: In a record, a meaningful collection of one or more related characters treated as a unit.

FIFO: A mnemonic for the operation of a queue first in, first out.

Fifth-generation Computers: Computers built since 1989 till now. They use large-scale integrated circuits, very fast and large main memory and disk storage, and very powerful programming languages and operating systems.

File: Collection of related records treated as a basic unit of storage. To handle files and distinguish between them, the files are to be named.

File Management System (FMS): A set of programmes provided to facilitate the users in organizing, creating, deleting, updating, and manipulating their files.

File Manager: The software integrated with the operating system capable of keeping, searching and name change of files.

File Processing: Keeping the file up-to-date by adding, changing, or deleting data.

File Roller: The Software in GNU/Linux to compress and decompress files.

File Transfer Protocol (FTP): An application level protocol, which allows a user to move a file from one computer to another in network environment.

File Utilities: A set of routines, which perform a variety of generalized operations (such as, sorting, searching, merging, copying, printing and maintenance) on data files.

Filtering: A utility in spreadsheet to extract information with respect to set parameters.

FIN: The final segment of a TCP transmission. Each side sends a FIN to close the connection.

Firewall: A software, which usually runs on the proxy server of an organization, and controls the flow of incoming and outgoing messages from within and organization for providing better security to the organization.

Firmware: A sequence of instruction (software), which is substituted for hardware, and stored in read-only memory (ROM).

First-generation Computers: Computes built between 1942 and 1955, which used vacuum tubes, and were programmed in assembly language. Few examples are ENIAC, EDVAC and EDSAC.

First-mover Advantage: The built-in advantage of being the first business in a particular category.

Fixed-head Magnetic Disk: A magnetic disk system, which that eliminate the use of an access mechanism by distributing all the read/write heads over the disk surfaces.

Fixed-wireless System: A wireless computing system, which supports little or no mobility of the computing equipment associated with the wireless network.

Flash Memory: A nonvolatile read/write random-access semiconductor memory in which data is stored as charge on the floating gate of a certain FET.

Flat Panel Displays: Computer displays whose thickness is much smaller than VDU. Normally used in Laptop computers. They use liquid crystal display technology. Emerging flat panel displays are Plasma displays and Field Emission displays.

Flip-flop: An electronic circuit, which can be placed in one out of two stable states. Each state may be used to represent a binary digit.

Floating Point Number: A number representation in which real numbers are expressed as a mantissa and an exponent. The mantissa is less than one. The exponent is an integer. The mantissa is multiplied by the base of the number raise to a power equal to the exponent. For example 44.86 in floating point is 0.4486E2 = 0.4486×10^2.

Floating Point Numbers: Signed numbers held in a fraction-exponent format. For example, 3216 would be represented as 0.321×10^4 in floating-point notation.

Floppy Disk: A small, round, flexible disk for storage of digital data. By inserting it into the floppy drive the data in the floppy disk can be transferred to the computer and vice versa. Also called diskette.

Floppy Disk Drive: A drive that facilitates reading from and writing on a floppy disk.

Flow: A set of packets headed for the same destination.

Flow Chart: A chart illustrating the logical sequence of events that must be performed to attain a pre-determined aim. It is a chart showing the sequence of steps needed in the programme for solving a problem with a computer.

Flow Control: A protocol mechanism that allows a receiver to control the rate at which a sender transmits data. Flow control makes it possible for a receiver running on a low-speed computer to accept data from a high-speed computer without being overrun.

Flowchart: A pictorial representation, which uses predefined symbols to describe either the logic of a computer programme (Programme Flowchart), or the data flow and processing steps of a system (system flowchart).

Flowcharting: The process of drawing a flowchart for an algorithm.

Folder: A portion of disk (hard or floppy) that we designate to store information. It may contain subfolders and files. It is also called directory.

Font: A collection of characters with predefined size and style.

For....Next: Command in BASIC for repeated application of an instruction.

Foreground Processing: Automatic execution of high-priority (foreground) jobs by preempting resources held by low-priority (background) jobs. Contrast with background processing.

Format: To prepare a floppy or hard disk for storing information.

Formatting Text: Some standard ways of representations of text. For example, one can put data in Times New Roman with font size 12 and font style as Italic or Bold.

Formula Bar: A box in the menu of spread sheet to specify the equation of a cell.

Formula Translation (FORTRAN): A high-level, programming language used for scientific and engineering applications.

Fortran: A high-level language; acronym for FORmula TRANSlator.

Forward: See store and forward.

Forward Bias: A voltage polarity condition that allows a semiconductor *pn* junction in a transistor or diode to conduct current.

Fourth-generation Computers: Computers built between 1975 and 1989. They used large-scale integrated circuits, semiconductor memories, and powerful high-level languages and operating systems.

FPGA: Filed programmable gate array; a type of PLD, consisting of an array of logic blocks with programmable row and column interconnecting channels surrounding by programmable I/O blocks.

FPM DRAM: Fast page mode dynamic random-access memory.

Fractional T1: A leased circuit that operates slower than T1 speed. Typically, factional T1 means 64 Kbps.

Fragment: A small IP datagram produced by fragmentation.

Fragmentation: The technique IP uses to divide a large datagram into smaller datagrams called fragments. The ultimate destination reassembles the fragments. See reassembly.

Frame: The form of a packet that the underlying hardware accepts and delivers.

Frame Relay: A Wide Area Network technology that provides connection-oriented service.

Framing Error: An error that occurs on asynchronous serial lines in which the receiver does not detect a valid frame (usually a character). Differences in the sender's and receiver's baud rate can cause framing errors.

Frequency (*f*): The number of pulses in one second for a period wave form. The unit of frequency is the hertz.

Frequency Division Multiplexing (FDM): A method used to concurrently transmit data between several transmitters and receivers over a single transmission medium. The available bandwidth of a physical medium is divided into smaller, disjoint, logical bandwidths, and each of the component bandwidths is used as a separate communications line (channel).

Front-end Processor: A processor designed specifically to handle the communications processing task. Its main purpose is to off-load communications processing task from the host computer, there by the host computer can be dedicated for applications and data processing jobs.

FSK: Frequency Shift Keying. A method of transforming digital signals 1 and 0 to two sine waves of different frequencies. This is done to transmit digital signals via an analog channel.

FTP (File Transfer Protocol): Abbreviation for File Transfer Protocol. It is one of the Internet services to retrieve and copy files from a remote computer.

FTTC (Fiber to the Curb): A technology proposed as a replacement for the existing cable television infrastructure that uses fiber optic trunks and a combination of coaxial cable and twisted pair to each subscriber.

Full Adder: An adder, which adds three binary digits and outputs a result bit and a carry bit.

Full Duplex: A data transmission mode in which data signals can be transmitted between a source and a destination in both directions simultaneously.

Full Duplex Communication: A method of using a communication channel in which signals can be transmitted between a source and a destination in both directions simultaneously.

Full-adder: A digital circuit that adds two bits and an input carry to produce a sum and an output carry.

Full-duplex Transmission: A communication between two computers in which data can flow in both directions at the same time. Full-duplex transmission requires two independent channels, one for data in each direction. See half-duplex transmission.

Function: A sub-programme, which returns a single value.

Function Keys: These keys can be programmed to do special jobs.

Functional Language: (Also known as Applicative language). Problems are solved suing this language by applying a sequence of functions to an input state to transform it to the required output state.

Functions Keys: Keys from F1 to F12 of a keyboard, which has specific function in application programmes (e.g. for Help press F1).

<font> HTML tag to regulate font, font size and colour.

Fuse: The programmable element in certain types of PLDs; also called a fusible link.

G

GAL: Generic array logic; an SPLD with a reprogrammable AND array, a fixed OR array, and programmable output logic macrocells.

Gallery: Online communication facility using a computer network.

Garbage-In-Garbage-Out (GIGO): Refers to computer errors caused due to incorrect input data, or unreliable programmes.

Gate: A logic circuit that performs a specified logic operation, such as AND or OR; one of the three terminals of a filed-effect transistor.

Gateway: (1) A computer, which is connected to the Internet by using a dedicated (leased) telephone line, and is used to provide Internet connectivity to other computers via it. (2) An internetworking tool, which is used to interconnect dissimilar networks that use different communication protocols.

GBPS (Giga Bits Per Second): A unit data transfer equal to *1000* Mbps or 10^9bps. See bps, Kbps, and Mbps.

Generation: In computer talk, it is step in technology. It provides a framework for the growth of the computer industry.

Generative Graphics: This deals with the creation of 2D and 3D pictures from the mathematical representation of the objects.

GEO (Geostationary Earth Orbit): A height for communication satellites that causes their orbit to match the rotation of the earth (approximately 36,000 kilometers or 20,000 miles). Also called Geosynchronous Earth Orbit. See LEO.

GIF (Graphics Interchange Format): A standard format for storing a graphics image. GIF images are especially popular on the World Wide Web.

Giga: A word used to represent $1024 \times 1024 \times 1024 = 2^{30} \approx 10^{9}$. Abbreviated form G.

Gigabit Ethernet: A version of Ethernet technology that operates at 1000 Mbps (i.e., 1 Gbps).

Gigabyte: Approximately on billion bytes.

Gigabytes (GB): Memory storage equal to 1,073,741,824 (2^{30}) bytes in a computer.

Gigaflop: 10^{9} floating-point arithmetic operations per second.

GIGO: 'Garbage In Garbage Out' is a term to express the condition that if a programme is not properly fed, then no results would be obtained.

Glitch: A voltage or current spike of short duration, usually unintentionally produced and unwanted.

Global Cell: A programmable cell in an SPLD array that affects all of the OLMCs when programmed.

Go To: Statement in BASIC that directs the computer to another statement.

Golf Ball: A small, removal metal sphere around the surface of which the characters of type are arranged.

Gradient Fill Tool: Tool to fill colour starting from one shade of another.

Graphic: Symbolic representation of concepts using lines and drawings except letters.

Graphic Tablets: An input device used for drawing on the monitor by putting pressure on a pad.

Graphical User Interface (GUI): An interface for computer users, which provides icons (pictures) and menus (list of choices), which users can select with a mouse for telling the computer what they want it to do for them.

Graphics: Is the representation of information by a computer in visual form.

Graphics Software: Software, which enables users to use a computer system for creating, editing, viewing, storing retrieving and printing designs, drawings, pictures, graphs, and anything else, which can be drawn in a traditional manner.

Gray code: An unweighted digital code characterized by a single bit change between adjacent code numbers in a sequence.

Gray Scales: The number of shades of colour that can be presented on a monochrome (black and white) monitor's screen, or on a monochrome printer's output.

Groupware: See computer supported co-operative working (CSCW).

GUI: Graphical User Interface. An interactive user interface that graphically displays information.

H

H. 323: An ITU standard for a family of protocols used with IP telephony (VoIP).

Hacker: A computer enthusiast who uses the computer as a source of recreation by pushing its capabilities to its limits (performance, security, storage, etc.).

Half Adder: An adder which adds two bits and gives the result bit and the overflow bit (if any).

Half Duplex: A communication system in which data can be transmitted between a source and a destination in both directions, but only in one direction at a time.

Half Duplex Channel: A communication channel in which signals may be transmitted at a time in only one direction from source to destination or vice-versa.

Half-adder: A digital circuit that adds two bits and produces a sum and an output carry. It cannot handle input carries.

Half-duplex Transmission: A communication between two computers in which data can flow in only one direction at a given time. Half-duplex transmission requires less hardware than full-duplex transmission because a single, shared physical medium can be used for all communication. See full-duplex transmission.

Hard Copy: The output on paper from a line-printer or teletype, etc. The soft copy is the copy stored in memory.

Hard Disk: A magnetic disk storage device, which uses disks made of rigid metal (frequently aluminium). The hard disk platters com in many sizes ranging from 1 to 14-inch diameter.

Hard Disk/Drive: Storage device permanently mounted inside a computer. Can store several million bytes of information.

Hard-copy Output: A computer output, which is permanent in nature and can be kept in paper files, or can be looked at a later time, when the person is not using the computer. For example, output produced by printers or plotters on paper.

Hardware: The circuitry and physical components of a computer system (as opposed to the directions called software).

Hardware Address: The address assigned to a computer that attaches to a network. A frame sent from one computer to another must contain the recipient's hardware address. A hardware address is also called a physical address or a MAC address.

Hashing: The process of using an address generating function (called hashing algorithm) to map a record's key field value to its storage address.

HDL: Hardware description language. ABEL and CUPL are examples.

HDSL (High-rate Digital Subscriber Line): A technology developed by the telephone companies to provide high speed digital service over local loop wiring. See ADSL.

Head-end Modem: A modem a telephone company or cable office. See tail-end modem.

Header: Repeated words such as page number, short version of the title or chapter name, paced at the top of a page for identification purpose.

Hecker: A person who can spend hours at a computer enjoy it.

Hertz: A unit of measure equal to an oscillation per second. Hardware bandwidth is measured in multiple of Hertz.

Heuristic: A general principle that often leads to the correct solution of a problem (often used in games such as chess etc.).

Hexadecimal: Describes a number system with a base of 16.

Hexadecimal Number System: A number system with a base of 16. Its digits range from 0 to F. It is commonly used as a shortcut notation for groups of four binary digits.

Hexadecimal System: A number system using 16 as base. The 16 symbols in this system are 0 to 9 and A, B, C, D, E, F.

HFC (Hybrid Fiber Coax): A replacement for the existing cable television infrastructure that uses optical fiber trunks with coaxial cable connections to each subscriber and provides two-way digital information transfer in addition to television signals. See cable mode.

Hidden Station Problem: A problem in wireless networks in which a third party can hear one but not both of a pair of communicating stations.

Hierarchical Addressing: An addressing scheme in which part of an address gives information about the location. For example, a telephone number is hierarchical because it begins with an area code followed by an exchange.

Hierarchical Database: A database model in which the data elements are linked in the form of an inverted tree structure with the root at the top and the branches formed below.

Hierarchical Network: A communications network in which computers or processors are connected in a tree-like structure.

High-level Language : A programming language whose structure is application oriented, and is independent of the structure of the computer. Each statement of such a language statements.

High-Z: The high-impedance state of a tristate circuit in which the output is effectively disconnected from the rest of the circuit.

Hold Time: The time interval required for the control levels to remain on the inputs to a flip-flop after the triggering edge of the clock in order to reliably activate the device.

Hollerith Code: A particular coding scheme used to present characters on 80-column punched cards.

Hologram: A photographic system which uses laser light to create a 3-D image.

Holographic: Mass storage of information on a film. The information is read with the help of laser.

Home Key: The key that moves the cursor to the beginning of a line.

Homepage: A document stored on a World Wide Web server that is the starting point for obtaining information about a particular individual, company, group, or topic. A homepage can contain pointers to additional pages of related information or to homepages for other topics.

Hop: A unit of measure used by Internet routing protocols. Each network counts as one hop.

Hop Count: A number in a protocol header that determines how many intermediate machines a packet visits. Protocols like IP require the sender to specify a maximum hop count; doing so prevents a packet from travelling around a routing loop forever.

Hop Limit: A synonym for hop count that is used by IPv6.

Hops: The number of routers a message must pass through to get to its intended recipient.

Host: A company that provides space for storing ("hosting") a Website.

Host: An end-users computer connected to a nework. In an internet, each computer is classified as a host or a router. See router.

Hotlist: A personal list of favourite URL addresses, which an Internet user is likely to frequently visit in future. A user's hotlist is automatically created and stored on his/her local web client computer by a browser.

House Keeping: A bit like spring cleaning, clearing up and organizing floppy space by getting rid of extraneous matter and files.

HTML (Hyper Text Markup Language): Short for Hyper Text Mark Up Language. The programming language used to create hypertext document for use on the World Wide Web.

HTML Editors: Software for each HTML page creation.

HTTP: Stands for Hypertext Transfer Protocol. This is a protocol through which hypertext pages are transmitted.

HTTPS (HTTP with Security): A version of HTTP that uses encryption to guarantee confidentiality.

Hub: A box to which unshielded twisted pair wires from the ethernet interfaces of computers are connected. It receives signals, reshapes and broadcasts them to all computers connected to it. CSMA/CD protocol is used.

Hung: A term often used when the computer suddenly stops functioning.

Hybrid Computer: A computer that combines the desirable features of both digital and analog computers; it accepts and processing both discrete and continuous data.

Hybrid Network: A network, which is a combination of two or more different network topologies.

Hydra Printers: Multifunctional devices, which perform the functions of two or more of the following office equipment—printer, fax machine, copy machine and scanner.

Hyper Link: Hyperlinks take viewers to other pages or other location on the same page in World Wide Web or interactive multimedia.

Hyper Media: A set of documents in which a given document can contain text, graphics, video and audio clips as well as embedded references to other documents. World Wide Web pages are hypermedia documents.

Hyper Text: A text format with facilities like Link, Bold, Italics etc. like and HTML file.

<head> HTML tag that indicate a head section.

<html> HTML tag that indicate a head section.

</html> HTML tag at the end of such a file.

Hyperlink: Interconnections of a Web of information.

Hyperlink: A technique to open another page from a webpage.

Hyperlink: A connection between one object and another; also known as a link. On a Web page, the line "www.mcgarvey.net" is a hyperlink that takes users to the author's Web page.

HyperText of Transport Protocol (HTTP): An Internet Protocol for interaction between the computers on the Internet.

Hysteresis: A characteristics of a threshold-triggered circuit, such as the Schmitt trigger, where the device turns on and off at different input levels.

I

I/O Ports: Sockets used to plug-in I/O devices to a computer system.

I/O Spooling: A technique in which the information to be read from slow input devices or those to be written on slow output devices are stored in a faster peripheral device such as a magnetic disk. Information is transferred to or from memory via this peripheral device.

I/O Units: Input/output units of a computer.

I/O-bound Jobs: Jobs whose CPU utilization is very low. They mostly perform I/O operations during the course of their processing.

I^2L: Integrated injection logic; an IC technology.

IANA (Internet Assigned Number Authority): The organization responsible for assigning numbers that the TCP/IP protocols use. For example, IANA assigns numeric values used in protocol header fields.

IBG: Inter Block Gap. The gap left in a magnetic tape store between blocks of data.

IBM Token Ring: An older local area Network technology developed by IBM Corporation that used a ring topology.

IC: Integrated Circuit. An electronic circuit fabricated on a single chip of silicon.

ICANN (Internet Corporation for Assigned Names and Numbers): The organization that sets policy for assignment of Internet addresses and domain names.

ICMP (Internet Control Message Protocol): The protocol that IP uses to report errors and exceptions. ICMP also includes informational messages used by programmes like ping.

Icon: A small picture on the screen often used in place of words. Many computer programmes display icons on the Desktop as shortcuts to execute certain commands or programmes or files.

Icon: A graphical object displayed on a visual display screen, which is used in place of words or phrases to allow users to select programme options, when selected with a mouse or other pointing device.

ICS (Internet Connection Sharing): The name of Microsoft's implementations of Network Address Translation. See NAT.

IDE Port: Port on motherboard to which Hard Disk, CD Drive, Floppy Drive etc. are connected.

IDL (Interface Definition Language): A specification language used with a remote procedure call mechanism.

IDS (Instruction Detection System): A security mechanism that watches packets arriving at a site and detects attacks.

IEEE: Institute of Electrical and Electronic Engineers.

IETF (Internet Engineering Task Force): The group that controls the TCP/IP protocol standards.

IF: Used to denote conditional statements in BASIC.

IF... Then: A statement in basic which specifies the operations to be carried out while a condition is true.

IGMP (Internet Group Multicast Protocol): The protocol a host uses to inform a router when it joins (or leaves) an Internet multicast group. IGMP is only used on a local network; a router must be another multicast routing protocol to inform other routers of group membership.

IGP (Interior Gateway Protocol): Term applied to any route propagation protocol used to transfer routing information within a single Autonomous Systems. See EGP.

IIS (Internet Information Server): Microsoft's name for their Web server product.

Image Processing: This deals with cleaning up blurred images and creating clear pictures.

Image Viewer: Software to watch pictures.

Immediate Addressing: An instruction in which the address part of an instruction is the operand and not the address of the operand.

Impact Printer: A matrix of dots forming the required characters that are created by the squirting of an ink jet. It is done at a high speed.

Impedance: The resistance of a cable to the transmission of signals; impedance is what accounts for signal attenuation.

Import: Transfer of data from one application to a currently running application.

Impress: A presentation software belonging to open Office Org.

Inbox: The folder in an e-mail programme containing received messages.

Increment: To increase the binary state of a counter by one.

Index Register: A register in CPU whose contents are added to the operand address specified in an instruction to find and effective address in memory from where the operand will be fetched.

Indexed Sequential Access Method (ISAM): See indexed sequential file.

Indexed Sequential File: A file organization in which an index (directory) file is used to have both sequential and random access to the records of the file. Also known as the indexed Sequential Access Method (ISAM).

Indirect Address: An instruction in which the address part of an instruction gives the address where the address of the operand would be found.

Information: Processed data obtained as the output of data processing. It is used by people to enhance understanding and to achieve specific purposes.

Information Retrieval: Recovering/getting information from storage media.

Information Technology: The application of appropriate technology to transmit, store and manipulate information to solve problems and make decisions.

Ink Jet Printer: Type of printer in which ink droplets are propelled using electrical signals to print letters and images.

INKEY$: A command in BASIC language.

Inkjet Printers: Character printers, which form characters and all kinds of images by spraying small drops of ink on to the paper.

Input: The data going into the computer and the process of putting in. The process of conveying information to a computer, usually through some mechanical device.

Input Command: An instruction to feed data to computer.

Input Device: A device used to enter data and instructions into a computer. Examples are keyboard, mouse, trackball, joystic, scanner, digitizer, voice recognition system, and vision input system.

Input File: The information entered in a computer that describes a logic design using a PLD programming language such as ABEL or CUPL; the part of an ABEL programme that contains declarations, logic descriptions, and test vectors.

Input Unit: A part of a computer used to feed programmes and data.

Input/Output (I/O) Devices: Machines used for transmitting (input)/ receiving (output) information from the computer.

Input/Output Register (I/O): A register, which is used to communicate with the input/output devices.

Insert: Options in a software for incorporating text, pictures or audio into a page.

Instruction: A command or order given to a computer. It normally consists of a code to indicate the operation to be performed, and address(es) in memory where the operand(s) would be found.

Instruction Register: A register in CPU which is used to store an instruction.

Instruction Register (I): A register, which holds the current instruction that is being executed.

Instruction Set: A set of machine instructions that the CPU has built-in ability to execute.

Instructions: Commands given to the computer for doing a specific job.

In-system Programming: A method for programming SPLDs after they are installed on a printed circuit board.

Integer: A whole number.

Integrated Circuit (IC): A type of circuit in which all of the components are integrated on a single chip of semi-conductive material of very small size.

Integrated Circuits (ICs): Circuits consisting of several electronic components like transistors, resistors, and capacitors grown on a single chip of silicon, eliminating wired interconnection between components.

Integrated Services Digital Network (ISDN): A telephone system, which provides digital (not analog) telephone and data services.

Intelligent Terminal: A terminal having extensive local processing capability. It has a built-in microcomputer, which can be programmed by users.

Inter Block Gap (IBG): When several records are in one block, these gaps separate the blocks of records on magnetic tape.

Interactive: Indicate communication and dialogue between the user sitting at a terminal and the computer.

Interface: A junction between two devices, i.e. a printer interface is the junction for the printer on the machine.

Interface Card: Special utility cards like Sound card, Network card etc. connected to the motherboard.

Interface Logic: Electronic circuit used to interconnect I/O devices to a computer's CPU or memory.

Interface Slot: Slot in motherboard to connect interface cards.

<i> HTML tag to represent a text in italics.

Interfacing: The process of making two or more electronic devices or systems operationally compatible with each other so that they function properly together.

Interference: The crossover that occurs when one type of signal or emission impinges on another, and either distort or diminishes it.

Interior Switch: A switch in a packet switched network that only connects to other packets switches, but not to host computers. See exterior switch.

Internal Storage: The addressable storage in a digital computer, which is directly under the control of the CPU.

Internet: A world wide network of computers. Several thousands of individual computer networks are interconnected to form the internet. Internet provides electronic mail, telnet (remote login to computer), file transfer services and enormous amount of information through various discussion groups and information retrieval facilities.

Internet Address: See IP address.

Internet Explorer: It is a software of Microsoft used for searching different sites in internet (Web browser of Microsoft).

Internet Firewall: A security mechanism placed at the connection between networks in an organization and networks outside the organization. The firewall restricts access to the organization's computers and services.

Internet Protocol: The TCP/IP conventions for transmitting data across a network.

Internet Reference Model: A set of networks and routers at a given organization using TCP/IP protocols to communicate. Usually, an organization's intranet connects to the global internet.

Internet Search Engine: An application available on the WWW, which helps users locate the websites containing useful information and references to such information.

Internet Service Provider (ISP): An organization, which maintains one or more gateway computers, and provides Internet access facility to other users by allowing them to connect their computers to its own gateway computer(s) by using a modem.

Internet Surfing: The process of navigating the Internet to search for useful information.

Internetwork Packet Exchange/Sequenced Packet Exchange (IPX/SPX): The set of protocols developed by Novell that is most commonly associated with NetWare, but is also supported in Microsoft networks.

Internetworking: Interconnecting of two or more networks to form a single network. The resulting network is called an internetwork.

Interoperability: Ability of diverse computers from different vendors with different operating systems to cooperate in solving computational problems.

Interpreter: A language processor, which translates a statement of a high-level language, and immediately executes it before translating the next source language statement. It is the most common language processor for BASIC.

Interrupt Service Routine: A computer programme stored in the compute which is invoked when an interrupt is sensed by CPU. This programme is usually used to transfer data from or to I/O devices to or from memory.

Interrupt Signal: A signal sent to the CPU by an external event such as when information from an input device is ready to be read.

Intranet: A network of computers within an organization which follows the same protocol as the internet and provides the same services as the internet.

IP: Stands for Internet Protocol. It is the protocol that ensures the passage of packets of information to the right destination.

IP Address: A 32-bit address assigned to a computer that uses TCP/IP protocols. The sender must know the IP address of the destination computer before sending a packet.

IP Datagram: The form of a packet sent across a TCP/IP internet. Each datagram contains two pieces: a header that identifies both the sender and receiver and payload area that contains the data being carried.

IP Switching: An effort to combine IP with hardware switching (especially ATM) to achieve higher speed. See layer-3 switching.

IP Telephony: The use of TCP/IP and the Internet for voice telephone calls. IP telephony involves signaling as well as the transmission of digitized voice. See VoIP.

IP Tunnel: A mechanism used to send a datagram (possibly one that is not routable) across the internet by encapsulating it in another IP datagram.

IP-In-IP: Term applied to the encapsulation used in an IP tunnel. An IP datagram is encapsulated in the payload area of another IP datagram for tranmission.

IPng (Internet Protocol-the Next Generation): The generic name used during early discussions of a new protocol to succeed IPv4. Researchers proposed several possible protocols for IPng. See IPv6.

IPsec (IP Security): A protocol that allows a sender to choose authentication or confidentiality for each datagram.

IPv4 (Internet Protocol Version 4): The version of IP currently used in the Internet. IPv4 uses 32-bit addresses.

IPv6 (Internet Protocol Version 6): A specific protocol that has been chosen by the IETF as a successor to IPv4. IPv6 uses 128-bit addresses.

ISC (International Softswitch Consortium): A consortium of vendors developing standards for IP telephony products.

ISCII (Indian Standard Code for Information Interchange): An 8-bit common code standardized by the Bureau of Indian Standards to represent characters of all Indian languages.

ISDN (Integrated Services Digital Network): Acronym for Integrated Service Digital Network. It is a fully digital line which can transmit data in any form, like text, image, voice, etc. over a telephone line.

ISO (International Organization for Standardization): The standards organization best known for having proposed the 7-layer reference model early in the history of data networking.

ISO Protocol: A communication protocol to interconnect geographically dispersed computers. This protocol has been standardized by the International Standards Organization.

ISO7: International Standards Organization 7-bit code.

Isochronous: A network engineered to deliver data with extremely low jitter. The voice telephone network is isochronous; most computer networks are not.

ISP (Internet Service Provider): Short for Internet Service Provider. A company that provides access to the internet.

Iteration Logic: A programme construct, which is used to produce loops in programme logic, when one or more instructions may be executed several times depending on some condition. Also known as looping logic.

Iterative Process: A method of performing a series of steps to produce successively better approximations to the solution of an equation or problem.

ITU (International Telecommunications Union): The organization that controls standards for telephone systems. The ITU also standardizes a few network technologies (e.g., ATM).

J

Jack: The clip like part of a connection cable of computer parts.

Jargon: A term used to refer to technical words which are not in every day use.

Java: A programming language defined by Sun Microsystems used to create active World Wide Web documents. Java programmes are compiled into a bytecode representation. After a browser a java programme, the programme runs locally to control the display.

JAVA: An object oriented language which is easily portable. It is normally used to programme computers connected in a network.

Java RMI (Java Remote Method Invocation): A middleware technology used with Java.

JavaScript: An interpretive language used for active World Wide Web documents. Because they are kept in source from, JavaScript programmes can be integrated with text in a World Wide Web page.

Jitter: A term that refers to the amount of variation in delay that a network introduces. A network with zero jitter takes exactly the same amount of time to transfer each packet, while a network with high jitter takes much longer to deliver some packets than others. Jitter is important when sending audio or video, which must arrive at regular intervals.

Job: See process.

Job Control Language: A special purpose language used to describe to a computer's operating system the resource requirements of programmes fed to the computer.

Job Control Language (JCL): A special purpose language, which is used to describe to computer's operating system the resource requirements of a job fed to the computer for processing.

Joystick: An input device, which serves as an effective pointing device for applications, such as video games, flight simulators, training simulators, and for controlling industrial robots.

JPEG (Joint Photographic Experts Group): A standard format for storing a graphics image. JPEG images are often used on the World Wide Web. The name is derived from the committee that published the standard.

. jpg: Extension part in the name of a file of picture.

JPEG-Joint Photographic Expert Group: A format for compressing digitalized still images.

JSP (Java Server Pages): A dynamic Web page technology intended to be platform-independent. Whenever the page is requested, the sever interprets Java code that is embedded in each page.

Jump: A technique used in programming to direct computer control from one section of the programme to another.

Jump Instruction: An instruction or signal, which, conditionally or unconditionally, specifies the location of the next instruction, and directs the computer to that instruction. A jump instruction is used to alter the normal sequence of control of the computer.

Justification: Alignment of text within margins of a page or in a textbox. It can be left, right, center, both left and right.

K

K: An abbreviation for Kilo, $1K = 2^{10} = 1024$.

Kbps (Kilo bits per second): A unit of data transfer equal to *1000* bits per second. See bps, Gbps, and Mbps.

Kernel: The central controlling part of an operating system, which implements the most primitive of the system's functions. It is the only part of an operating system, which a user cannot replace or modify.

Key Field: A unique field in a record, which is used to distinguish one record from another.

Keyboard: Is a group of buttons on a pad used to input information into a computer system manually. A computer keyboard consists of the standard typewriter keys, numeric key pad and function keys.

Key-to-disk: A process in which data are transmitted from a key board to a magnetic/floppy disk.

Key-to-tape: A device used to enter data onto a magnetic tape.

Keyword: A word defined by the language; a keyword gives a certain specific information to the compiler.

Kilo: Used to represent $1024 = 2^{10}$ in computers. Abbreviated form K.

Kilobytes (KB): Memory storage equal to 1024 (2^{10}) bytes in a computer.

Kimball Tag: A turn around document in the form of a miniature punched card, particularly used in garment retailing.

Kiosk: An unattended system, which is used to store information of public interest, and allows common people to access the stored information as per their requirement.

K_u-Band Transmission: The use of 11 Gh_z to 14 Gh_z band of frequencies for transmission and retransmission of microwave signals in a satellite communication system.

L

Label : One or more characters used to identify a statement, an instruction, or a data field in a computer programme.

Label Record: A machine-readable record, which is used to identify a data file. It is the first record of the file.

Label Switching: A technique used by switching technologies such as ATM in which each switch that handles a cell rewrites the cell's label.

Lan: Short for Local Area Network. A network used to interconnect computers in a building or a campus.

LAN (Local Area Network): A network that uses technology designed to span a small geographic area. For example, an Ethernet is a LAN technology suitable for use in a single building. LANs have lower propagation delay than WANs or MANs. See MAN and WAN.

Landscape Mode: A mode of printing in which the printed lines are parallel to the longer edge of the paper.

Language: A set of rules and conventions used to convey information.

Language Processor: A software used to convert source programme instructions to object or machine language instructions. Few examples are assembler, compiler and interpreter.

Lap Top Computer: A portable computer that can be used on lap.

Laptop (or Notebook) Computers: A portable computer which weighs around 2 kg and runs all PC applications. It uses a liquid crystal display and is usable by a person while travelling.

Large Scale Integration (LSI): A device used to measured the circuit density of a chip. Generally, it is measured in thousands of gates.

Laser: Light amplification by stimulated emission of radiation. A system of tuning light waves so that they form a very strong and narrow beam of light.

Laser Disk: See optical disk.

Laser Printers: Page printers, which produce very high quality output by forming characters and all kinds of images with very tiny ink particles. They use a combination of laser-beam and electrophotographic techniques to create printed outputs.

Latency: In case of disk storage, the relational delay time for the desired data (sector) to come under the read/write head positioned over that track. Maximum latency time equals the time taken by disk to rotate once.

Latency Time: The time taken for a record stored in a disk track (which is to be read) to come under the read/write head positioned over that track. Maximum latency time equals the time taken by disk to rotate once.

Layer : A technique applied to prepare picture files.

Layer Box: Dialog box showing details of layers in a picture file.

Layer Model: A conceptual framework to explain the purpose and interaction among a set of protocols. Layering is primarily beneficial to protocol designers; once implemented, protocols can be used without understanding layering.

5-layer Reference Model: A conceptual model that explains how TCP/IP Internet protocols are designed.

7-layer Reference Model: An early conceptual model devised by the International Organization for Standardization to specify how a set of protocols work together to provide communication services. The 7-layer model did not include an internet protocol layer.

802.1x: An IEEE standard for a security mechanism used with wireless networks.

802.2: The IEEE standard for Logical Link Control. See LLC and SNAP.

802.3: The IEEE standard for Ethernet.

802.5: The IEEE standard for a Wi-Fi wireless network.

Layer-3 Switching: An effort to combine IP with hardware switching (especially ATM) to achieve high speed. See IP switching.

Layout: The overall style of arrangement of matter, pictures and letter in a page.

Leaf: Lowest element in a hierarchical database structure.

Leased Line: A data transmission service in which a special conditioned telephone line directly and permanently connects two computers. A leased line can be used for both voice and data transmission. Also known as private line or dedicated line.

Left Click: Clicking on the left button of the mouse. When not otherwise specified, clicking means left clicking.

Left Mouse Button: The button on the left side of the mouse..

LEFT$: Function in BASIC to show the left letter in a string.

LEN: Function in BASIC to show the size of a string.

LEO (Low Earth Orbit): A height for communication satellite in which one orbit takes approximately 90 minutes. See GEO.

LET: Command in BASIC to give the value of square.

Let: Instruction in BASIC to fix the value of a variable.

LEX: A tool used to perform lexical analysis of a programming language.

Lexical Rules: Rules to specify syntactic elements or words of a programming language.

Library Function: A pre-defined function; normally supplied as part of the language compiler.

Library Routine: A tested routine maintained in a library of programmes.

Light Pen: A device which, when placed against a monitor screen, can be tracked by the computer. It is used to select data on the monitor and sometimes to trace information as input to a programme.

Lightweight Directory Access Protocol (LDAP): Part of the TCP/IP protocol suite, LDAP is a set of protocol for accessing information directories.

Line: Instruction in BASIC to draw a line.

Line Conditioning: A method in which special circuits are added at both ends of a leased analog telephone line to compensate for unequal attenuation and delay of different frequencies. This ensures digital signals to be sent reliably on an analog telephone line.

Line Driver: An electronic amplifier used to increase the power of a digital signal to be transmitted over a communication line.

Link: Communication channel between two systems or devices.

Linker: A programme, which is used to properly combine all the object programme files (modules) of a software, and to covert them into the software's final executable form.

Link-state: Synonym for link-status.

Link-status: An algorithm that routers use to compute optimal routes to each destination. Each router receives information about the status of network links, and uses the information in a shortest-path computation. See Dijkstra's algorithm, distance-vector, and SPF.

Linux: A free operating system developed by Linus Torwalds, got popularized as GNU/Linux by collaboration with GNU of free software foundation established by Richard Stalman.

LISP: A List Processing language. This high level language is used in applications such as theorem proving, game playing, etc.

LISt Processing (LISP): A programming language suitable for manipulating non-numeric data, such as symbols and strings of text. It is used in the areas of pattern recognition, artificial intelligence, and for simulation of games.

LLC (Logical Link Control): Part of IEEE LLC/SNAP header used to identify the type of a packet. The entire header is 8 octets, with the LLC portion occupying the first three. Seen SNAP.

Load Module: The final executable form of a software produced by a linker.

Loader: It is a system programme which accepts a linked object programme produced by a linker and loads it in the memory ready for execution.

Local Area Network (LAN): A computer network, which interconnects computers and other peripheral devices within a limited geographical area of a few kilometers.

Local Loop: A term that telephone companies use to refer to the wiring between the central office and a subscriber (e.g., an individual business or residence). A variety of technologies have been developed to provide high-speed digital services over existing local loop wiring. See ADSL and HDSL.

Locality of Reference: A term used to express the idea that communication tends to follow patterns. Spatial locality or reference means that a computer is more likely to communicate with a nearby computer than a distant computer, and temporal locality of reference means that a computer is more likely to communicate with the same computer repeatedly than to communicate with a new computer each time.

Log : A record of all visits to a Website; a log usually gives a click-by-click report on a visitor.

Logic: A system of reasoning where a particular set of inputs will predictably produce a particular set of outputs.

Logic Circuit: See combinational circuit.

Logic Error: An error, which occurs when the actual logic of a programme is different from the desired logic. Such errors cause the programme to produce incorrect output.

Logic Gate: An electronic circuit, which operates on one or more input signals to produce standard output signals. For example, AND, OR and NOT gates. Logic gates are the building blocks of all the circuits in a computer.

Logical Link Control (LLC): One of the two sublayers of the Data-Link layer of the OSI model. LLC moves packets onto and off of the network.

Logical Operators: Symbols used to show a logical relations between two data items. Examples in FORTRAN are EQ. For equal, and GT. For greater than.

Login/Logon: Method of entry into a computer facility by using a password.

Logo: A programming language specifically designed for teaching children to create little designs using a computer. It contains an imaginary turtle which is controlled by Logo commands/ instructions.

Logo Procedures: A set of instructions/commands defined to do certain task, e.g., drawing a square with Logo.

Logoprimitive: A Logo primitive is a basic Logo command.

Long-haul Network: Synonym for WAN.

Look-to-buy Ratio: A common metric (or measurement) used in analyzing the effectiveness of an e-tailer. Ideal would be 1 to 1—one looker produces one buyer. Most e-tailers are happy with look-to-buy ratios well under 10 to 1.

Loop: A sequence of instructions, which is executed repeatedly, until a terminal condition occurs.

Loopback Address: An IP address with 127 in the first octet that cannot be used as the host address on a network. It is used to test the TCP/IP protocol stack within a computer without sending information out onto the network.

Looping Logic: See iteration logic.

Low-level Languages: Programming languages, which normally translate from one source instruction to one object instruction. These languages are machine dependent.

LSI: A Large Scale Integrated circuit. An electronic circuit with about 10,000 transistors fabricated on a silicon chip.

M

MAC Address (Medium Access Control Address): An address, such as an Ethernet address, that is part of the MAC layer.

Machine Code: The pattern of binary bits stored in computer that indicate and cause the performance, when quoted, of specific machine functions. It is the computer's own language of 0s and 1s.

Machine Independent Language: A high level programming language which is designed to be used with a variety of computers.

Machine Language: A low-level language, which is directly understandable by the computer system. Each model of a computer has a unique machine language.

Machine Readable Form: Information which can be read by input devices connected to a computer.

Macro: A sequence of frequently used operators, or keystrokes bundled together as a single command, or keystroke by software, so that the invocation of the single command or keystroke leads to the invocation of all the operations/ keystrokes in the specified sequence. This helps speed user interaction with the system.

Macro Flowchart: A flow chart which outlines the main segments of a programme, or shows less detail.

Macro Instruction: An instruction in a source language, which is equivalent to a specified sequence of machine instructions.

Magnetic Core: A tiny ring shaped piece of magnetic material that is used to store data in the main computer memory.

Magnetic Disk: See disk.

Magnetic Ink Character Recognition (MICR): A technology used by the banking industry for faster processing of the large volume of cheques. This technology also ensures accuracy of data entry, because most of the information is pre-printed on the cheque and is directly fed to the computer.

Magnetic Storage: Storage devices such as disks, drums, tapes, cores, etc., which utilize the magnetic properties of materials to store data.

Magnetic Storage: Storing data utilizing the magnetic properties of materials; magnetic storage devices are disks, drums, cores, tapes, cassettes, films and magnetic cards, etc.

Magnetic Tape: A secondary storage device, which uses a long plastic strip coated with a magnetic material as a recording medium.

Magneto Resistive Head: Heads used to read data from magnetic disks. They depend on the change of resistance of head when a magnet is taken near it. They are more sensitive compared to traditional inductive coil heads.

Magneto-optical Disk: A storage disk, which integrates optical and magnetic disk technologies to enable rewritable storage with lager-beam technology.

Mail Exploder: A programme used to forward e-mail message. A mail exploder consults a database to determine how to handle each message. The name arises because a mail exploder may send copies of a message to multiple recipients if the database specifies many recipients for a given address.

Main Memory: The internal memory of a computer.

Mainframe: A large computer of which the peripherals are mounted in a frame.

Mainframe Computers: Large computers used by organizations such as banks. They process hundreds of millions of transactions per second, have hundreds of gigabytes of disks and very fast data transfer rate between disk and main memory. They can be accessed simultaneously by hundreds of terminals.

Mainframe System: A computer system, which is mainly used for handling the bulk of data and information processing of such organizations as banks, insurance companies, hospitals, railways, etc. They are also used in such environments where a large number of users need to share a common computing facility, such as in research groups, educational institutions, engineering firms, etc.

MAN (Metropolitan Area Network): A network that uses technology designed to span a city. MANs have higher propagation delay than LANs. See LAN and WAN.

Management Information System (MIS): An organized collection of people, procedures, and devices used to provide the right information to the right person at the right time for proper decision-making.

Manchester Encoding: The physical layer encoding that Ethernet uses to transmit a frame.

Manufacturer-programmed ROM: A ROM in which data is burnt in by manufacturer of the electronic equipment in which it is used.

Markup: Representation of a commands using special symbols like tag.

Mask: See address mask.

Masquerade: The name of a Linux programme that implements Network Address Translation. See NAT.

Mass Storage: Storage systems, which provide access to several terabytes of stored data. They use multiple units of storage media (such as multiple disks, multiple tapes, multiple CD-ROMs) as a single secondary storage device.

Massively Parallel Processing (MPP): An approach to designing supercomputers in which thousands of processors are integrated within a single computer, so that the supercomputer can peforme thousands of tasks simultaneously.

Master File: A file containing relatively permanent data. This file is often updated by records in a transaction file.

Mathematica: A problem oriented language used to simplify complex algebraic expression symbolically. Also used for indefinite integration.

MATLAB: A problem oriented language used by scientists and engineers to solve algebraic and differential equations.

Maximize: Title bar button to enlarge window size to the maximum.

Maximize Button: A button by which a software/window under use can be maximized.

Maxterm: A Boolean quantity consisting of all terms (in its normal form or complement form) Ored together. Any combination (2^n for n variables) of terms and complements is permissible, provided all are included in the term.

MBONE (Multicast backBONE): An experimental system used to send multicast data across the Internet. Although MBONE routers multicast locally, they use an IP tunnel to transfer multicast datagrams across the Internet from oen site to another.

MBPS (Megabits Per Second): A unit of data transfer equal to 10^6 bps. See bps, Gbps, and Kbps.

MCU (Multipoint Control Unit): A hardware unit used with IP telephony to handle conference calls.

Media: The actual cable (or radio or microwaves in wireless networking) used to transmit data over the network.

Media Access Control (MAC): One of the two sublayers of the Data –Link layer of the OSI model. MAC moves packets onto and off of the network.

Media Player: A software in Windows to watch movies.

Medium Scale Integration (MSI): A circuit with about 100 transistors fabricated on a single chip.

Mega: Used to represent $1024 \times 1024 = 2^{20} \cong 10^6$. Abbreviated form M.

Megabyte: It is approximately 1,000,000 bytes of data.

Megabytes (MB): Memory storage equal to 1,048,576 (2^{20}) bytes in a computer.

Memory: The chips in the computer where information and instructions are stored in binary code. Refers to the internal storage capacity of the central processor. Also known as an immediate access store. Memory Data Register (MDR): A special register which holds all data instructions temporarily as the pass in and out of main memory.

Memory Address Register (MAR): A register, which holds the address of the active memory location and loaded from the programme control register when an instruction is read from memory.

Memory Buffer Register (MBR): A register, which holds the contents of the memory word read from, or written in, memory.

Memory Cell : A circuit which can store data. A binary memory cell would store a 0 or a 1.

Memory Dump: Contents of memory duplicated on another storage device or printed on a printer.

Memory Map: A diagrammatic summary of the apportioning of space in the main memory for systems software and user programmes.

Memory Partition: In a multiprogramming system, the area occupied by each job residing simultaneously in the main memory.

Memory Slot: Part of a motherboard to connect memory cards.

Menu: These are means for presenting a list of choices e.g. File, Edit, View, etc. are menus in a programme.

Menu Bar: A menu in which the options are displayed on a horizontal bar (usually at the tope of the display screen) displayed across the screen.

Merge: Process of unification of two or more cells in a spread sheet.

Merging: The combining of records from two or more ordered files into a single ordered file.

Mesh: A hybrid in which all computers are connected to each other to provide fault-tolerant connections throughout a network.

Mesh Network: A network architecture in which a computer has a point-to-point connection to other computer(s). Full mesh networks, in which each pair of computers is directly connected, offer the highest throughput but are uncommon because they are expensive and difficult to change. See bus topology and ring topology.

Message Switching: A data communication method in which the data (message) to be sent is first appended with the destination address, and then sent across the network to its destination.

Meta Tag: An HTML expression that defines a Website's content, to be read by search engines and crawlers.

Metropolitan Area Network (MAN): Networks, which share some of the characteristics of both LANs and WANs. They usually interconnect computes spread over a geographical area of about 50 kilometers.

MGCP (Media Gateway Control Protocol): A system used for call setup between an IP telephone system and the PSTN.

MIB (Management Information Base): A set of named items that an SNMP agent understands. To monitor or control a remote computer, a manager must fetch or store values to MIB variables.

MICR: Acronym for Magnetic Ink Character Recognition. It reads by sensing shapes printed with magnetic ink.

Micro: Used to represent 10^{-6}.

Micro Computer: A computer that works based on a single microprocessor. All PCs are micro computers.

Micro Flowchart: A flowchart with more details. It is also called a detailed flowchart.

Microcode: The very basic directions, which tell the CPU how to execute an instruction; located in the control unit.

Microcomputer: A small computer, based on microelectronic technology. A computer is based on a microprocessor, while a microcomputer usually means a complete microcomputer system with input, output and storage. The word is sometimes used for the actual microprocessor chip.

Microcontroller: An inexpensive special purpose microprocessor which is optimized for control applications. It has an in-built ROM to store control programmes and also has built-in I/O controller.

Microfiche: Visual aid which exposes microfilms to very large scale.

Microkernel: A very small machine dependent core of an O.S. which coordinates the activities of device drivers, file server, scheduler and memory manager.

Microphone: Device connected to a computer that accepts sound as an input.

Microprocessor: A silicon chip which can do the same jobs as the main parts inside a computer. It is normally used to mean the single chip containing the central processing unit, but it can also be used to mean the complete microcomputer system.

Microprogramme: Firmware programmes residing in read-only memory (ROM). They deal with low-level machine functions, and are essentially substitutes for additional hardware.

Microsecond: One-millionth of a second, 1 microsecond = 10^{-6} sec.

MID$: Function in BASIC to find the middle letter in a string.

Middleware: A set of tools that helps a programmer build client-server software. Each middleware technology is designed for a specific programming language. See RMI and RPC.

Mill: Another word for a processor.

Milli: Used to represent 10^{-3}.

Millisecond: One-thousand of a second, 1 millisecond= 10^{-3} sec.

Milometer (Odometer): An instrument that records the distance a scooter or a motor vehicle has covered.

MIME (Multipurpose Internet Mail Extensions): A mechanism that allows nontext data to be sent in a standard Internet e-mail message. A MIME sender encodes data using printable characters: a MIME reader decodes the message.

Mind Share: Consumer awareness and loyalty.

Mini Computer: A computer bigger than a microcomputer and smaller than a main frame computer.

Minicomputer: A relatively small (bigger than a microcomputer) but fast computer with somewhat limited input/output capabilities.

Minimize: Reducing a window to the form of an icon in the task bar. When the mouse pointer is clicked on this, the window assumes the original size.

Minimize Button: A button for reducing a window to the form of an icon. When the mouse pointers is clicked on this icon, the window assumes its original size.

Minterm: A Boolean quantity consisting of all terms (in its normal form or complement form) ANDed together. Any combination (2^n for n variables) of terms and complements is permissible, provided all are included in the term.

MIPS: Millions of Instruction Per Second.

Mnemonic: Any kind of a mental trick we use to help us remember. For example, a computer may be designed to interpret the machine code of 1111 (binary) as the subtract operation, but it is easier for a human being to remember it as SUB.

Mobile Computing: A wireless computing system, which supports mobility of the computing equipment, which the users use to access the resources associated with the wireless network. It allows mobile users to access information from anywhere and at anytime. Also known as nomadic computing.

MOD: Function in Basic to calculate balance.

Modem (Modulator/DEModulator): A device that encodes digital information in a carrier wave for transmission across copper wires or a dialup telephone connection. A pair of modems permits two-way communication because each modem contains circuitry to encode outgoing data and decode incoming data. See DSU/CSU.

Modems: Modulators-Demodulators. Found at the end of analog devices, they are used to translate between digital pulses and analog waves. They connect things like the telephone to the computer.

Modulation: The process of changing a carrier wave (usually a sine wave) to encode information. The frequency of the carrier and the modulation technique determining the rate at which data can be sent.

MOdulator-DEModulator (Modem): Devices used to convert digital signals (to be communicated over an analog channel, such as telephone line) to analog form at the sending end, and back to digital form at the receiving end.

Monitor: A display device (like TV) used for display of computer input and output.

Monitor: Something which keeps a check on something else; or in the computer system, a screen to display the computer's information.

Moore's Law: A prediction that the number of transistors in a microprocessor will double every 18 months.

MOSFET: Metal Oxide Silicon Field Effect Transistor. This is used as an electronic switch.

MOSPF (Multicast Extensions OSPF): A multicast routing protocol that extends OSPF to handle multicast.

Motherboard: The main circuit board of a computer system. It has the CPU chip, RAM chips, ROM chips, I/O handling chips, etc. mounted on it. Also known as system board.

Mouse: A palm-sized button operated pointing device that can be slid on a spherical wheel. It is used to control movement of cursor on the screen, selection and implementation of commands, etc. It may have two or three buttons.

Mouse Pad: A flat piece of material which provides a smooth surface to mouse for scrolling.

Mouse Pointer: Little symbol on the screen whose movement is controlled by the mouse.

Move Tool: Tool to change the position of a picture.

Movie File: Common name of a movie or video file.

MP3: MPEG-Layer 3. A file format for compressing digitized audio files.

MPEG: Motion Picture Coding Expert Group. A committee of International Standard Organization which develops format for compressing digitized audio/video files.

MPEG 4 (Moving Pictures Experts Group version 4): A standard format for digital video and audio that allows the two streams to be synchronized (i.e., played together). The name is derived from the committee that published the standard.

Mplayer: Software in GNU/Linux to watch movie or video clippings.

MPLS (MultiProtocol Label Switching): A connection-oriented networking technology that uses label switches.

Mrouted (Multicast Route Daemon): A UNIX programme that performs multicast routing. Mrouted implements the DVMRP protocol, and is used in the MBONE.

MS-DOS: Stands for Microsoft Disk Operating System. A single-user operating system, which was popularly used for personal computers in the 1980s.

MSI: Medium Scale Integrated Circuit. A circuit with about 1000 transistors fabricated on a single silicon chip.

MS-WINDOWS: An operating system with a good graphical user interface and multitasking facility developed by Microsoft Corporation for PCs.

MTU (Maximum Transmission Unit): The largest amount of data that can be sent across a given network in a single packet. Each network technology defines an MTU (e.g., the MTU of an Ethernet is 1500 octets).

Multi-access Bus Network: A network in which a single transmission medium is shared by all nodes.

Multicast: A form of addressing in which a set of computers is assigned one address; a copy of any datagram sent to the address is delivered to each of the computers in the set. Often used for audio or video conferences. See broadcast, cluster, and unicast.

Multihomed: Any host computer that attaches to more than one network. In most protocol systems, a multihomed computer has more than one address.

Multimedia: A programme combining text, audio, video, graphics, pictures, voice, etc.

Multimedia: Technique to include sound and visual.

<marquee> HTML tag to move a text on a page.

Multimedia Computer System: A computer system, which has the capability to integrate two or more types of media (text, graphics, animation, audio, and video) for the purpose of generation, storage, representation, manipulation and access of multimedia information.

Multimedia KIT: Devices like CD-ROM, DVD, Sound Card, Speaker and Microphone used for multimedia facilities.

Multiplex: A general concept that refers to combining independent sources of information into a form that can be transmitted over a single communication channel. Multiplexing can occur both in hardware (i.e., electrical signals can be multiplexed) and in software (i.e., protocol software can accept message sent by multiple application programmes and send them over a single network to different destinations). See demultiplex.

Multiplexing: The method of dividing a physical channel into many logical channels, so that a number of independent signals may be simultaneously transmitted on it.

Multiprocessing: A term used to describe interconnected computer configurations, or computers with two or more independent CPUs, which have the ability to simultaneously execute several programmes.

Multiprocessor: A computer system consisting of two or more CPUs under a common control.

Multiprogramming: Interleaved execution of two or more different and independent programmes by the same computer.

Multiprogramming Operating System: An operating system in which a number of programmes are kept in memory and CPU and I/O resources are dynamically allocated to programmes with the objective of keeping all the units of a computer simultaneously active.

Multitasking: Executing multiple programmes residing in memory concurrently in a CPU. Each task is allocated a time slice to use CPU.

N

Nano: Used to represent 10^{-9}.

Nanosecond: One-billionth of a second, 1 nanosecond = 10^{-9} sec.

NAPT (Network Address and Port Translation): The most common form of address translation in which protocol port numbers are translated as well as IP addresses. See NAT.

Narrowband Channel: Communication channels, which handle low volumes of data, typically from 45 to 300 baud. They are used mainly for telegraph lines and low speed terminals.

NAT (Network Address Translation): A technology that provide connectivity for many computers at a site through a single valid IP address. NAT rewrites the header of each outgoing and incoming datagram to replace the internal address with the globally valid IP address and vice versa. See NAPT.

Nautilus: File manager in Linux.

NBMA (Non Broadcast Multiple Access): Characteristic of a network technology that connects multiple computers but does not support broadcast. ATM is an example of an NBMA network.

Netiquette: Deals with the rules of framing messages while interacting with other internet users.

Network: A group of computers (and printer) connected to share information/resources and to communicate with each other.

Network Access Point (NAP): A part of the Internet backbone where Internet service providers (ISPs) share ··iting and addressing information in a peering arrangement.

Network Adapter: Synonym for NIC.

Network Analyzer: A device that listens to a network, usually a LAN, in promiscuous mode and reports on traffic. Also called a network monitor.

Network Card: An add-on card to network computers.

Network Database: A database model in which the data elements are recognized in the form of parent-child relationships.

Network Interface Card (NIC): A hardware device, which allows a computer to be connected to a network, both functionally and physically.

Network Layer: Layer 3 of the OSI networking model that is responsible for assigning a globally unique address to every device and providing directions from any point on the neetwork to any other point. To achieve this routed and routing protocols operate at this layer.

Network Management: A reference to the job of administering, monitoring, and controlling a network. Protocols like SNMP automate some of the monitoring and control tasks.

Network Monitor: A synonym for network analyzer.

Network Operating System (NOS): A software collection that allows a computer to communicate on a network.

Network Topology: The structure of interconnection of nodes of a computer network.

Newsgroup: A group of Internet/Intranet users, who use the usenet facility of the Internet to exchange their views/ideas/ information on some common topic, which is of interest to all the group members.

Newsgroup: An internet message board, or bulletin board.

Next Geader: A field in an IPv6 header that specifies the type of the next item.

Next-hop Forwarding: The technique used by protocols like IP to forward a packet to its final destination. Although a given router does not contain complete information about the path a datagram will follow, the router does know the next router to which the datagram should be sent.

NFS (Network File System): A remote file access mechanism originally defined by Sun Microsystems for use with the UNIX operating system. NFS allows applications on one computer to access files on a remote computer.

Nibble: A unit of four bits. Half a byte.

NIC (Network Interface Card): A hardware device that plugs into a computer and connects the computer to a network. Often called a network adapter.

NIU (Network Interface Unit): The piece of equipment that the telephone company supplies to terminate a digital circuit. See demarc and NTI.

Node: A term used informally to refer to a router or a computer attached to a network. The term is derived from graph theory.

Nomadic Computing: See mobile computing.

Nonimpact Printer: A printer, which performs some type of operation to the paper, instead of physically striking it (as in the case of an impact printer). To print characters with nonimpact printers, the paper can be sprayed with ink, magnetized, electrically charged, heated, placed under pressure, or struck by laser beams.

Non-positional Number System: A number system in which each symbol represents the same value, regardless of its position in the number, and the symbols are simply added to find out the value of a particular number. It is very difficult to perform arithmetic with such a number system.

Nonvolatile: A storage medium that retains its contents when the electric power is switched off.

Non-volatile Storage: A storage medium, which retains its contents when the power is turned off or interrupted.

Normalized Floating Point Number: A floating point number in which the most significant digit of the mantissa is made non-zero.

Note Pad: An application software for crating text files.

Notebook Computer: A small, portable compute mainly for use by people who need computing power wherever they go.

NTI (Network Terminating Interface): The piece of equipment that the telephone company supplies to terminate a digital circuit. See demarc and NIU.

Number Cruncher: An expression used when the application requires very complicated computations.

Numeric: Pertaining to a character set, which contains the numbers 0 to 9.

Numeric Character : A character belonging to one of the digits 0-9.

Numeric Key Pad: A special set of numeric key on a computer keyboard, which allows faster keying in of numeric data.

Numerical Control (NC): A system for controlling machinery by feeding a series of numbers, usually on paper tape.

Nyquist Sampling Theorem: A mathematical result from information theory that specifies the number of samples that must be taken to digitize and then reconstruct a wave. The sampling theorem applies to sending audio over a network.

Nyquist's Intersymbol Interference Theorem: A mathematical result from information theory that specifies an upper bound on the maximum rate at which data can be sent. See Shannon's Theorem.

O

Object: A programming model to represent a real world object. All the necessary data structures and procedures needed to model it are encapsulated. An object is invoked by sending a message to it requesting its services.

Object Linking and Embedding (OLE): A feature found in application software packages, which allows joining of documents in different applications, so that change in either document are reflected in the other document.

Object Oriented Language: A programming language having facilities to model objects and methods to invoke objects.

Object Programme: A fully compiled or assembled programme, which is ready to be loaded into the computer. It results from the translation of a source programme by a language processor.

Object-oriented Database: A database model, which captures object-oriented concepts, such as class hierarchy, inheritance, and methods.

Object-Oriented Programming (OOP): A pro-gramming methodology, which deals with solving problems by identifying the real-world objects of the problem and the processing required of those objects, and then creating stimulations of those objects, their processes, and the required communications between the objects.

Object-oriented programming languages: Programming languages, which encapsulate data and sequences of operations into abstract entities called objects, providing a stronger encapsulation mechanism than procedure. Hence, object-oriented programming provides a more powerful modeling tool than procedure-oriented programming.

OC (Optical Carrier): A set of standards adopted by common carriers for the high-speed transmission of digital information over optical fiber. OC-1 operates at 51.840 Mbps; OC-*n* runs at *n* times that bit rate. See STS.

OC-3 (Optical Carrier 3): A standard for the optical fiber encoding used in popular telephone company digital circuits. An OC-3 circuit operates at 155.520 Mbps. See OC.

Octal Number System: A number system with a base of 8. The octal digits range from 0 to 7. It is commonly used as a shortcut notation for groups of three binary digits.

Octal System: A number system whose base is 8.

Odd Parity: A parity bit added to a unit of data, usually each character, to make the number of *I* bits odd. A receiver checks the parity to determine whether data has been corrupted during transmission. See even parity.

Off-line: A device or system not directly under the control of a computer system.

Off-line Data Entry Devices: Input devices through which data is recorded on some media, such as floppies or tapes, and then entered later into the computer from the media form processing.

OMR: Stands for Optical Mark Recognition. It reads position of marks on a paper and then inputs to computer.

One-arm Router: Term used informally to define a computer that only has one network interface, but has been configured to behave like a router. One-armed routers are often used with Network Address Translation. See NAT and router.

On-line: It is the state of being connected. For example for surfing the Internet we have to be on-line to the Internet.

On-line Data Entry Devices: Input devices, which are connected directly to the computer on which the entered data is processed.

On-line System: A computer system which has terminals connected to it and allows direct access to user files from terminals. The files are updated as soon as a transaction is completed.

Open: To start a programme or display/present content of a file.

Open Shortest Path First (OSPF): A part of the TCP/IP protocol suite, OSPF is a link-state routing protocols that determines the best path for a packet through an internetwork.

Operand: The part of a machine level instruction, which tells the central processor the location of the data to be manipulated.

Operating System: An integrated set of programmes, which controls the resources of a computer system, and provides its users with an interface or virtual machine, which is more convenient to use than the bare machine.

Operation Code: A group of bits used to represent operations to be performed by a CPU.

Operation Code (Op Code): The part of a machine level instruction which tells the central processor what has to be done.

Operation Phase: The life-cycle phase during which the system constructed in the development phase is used.

Optical Bar Reader: The devices which read bar codes (usually series of black and white lines on the packing of the products) and translates the information into digital form.

Optical Bar-code Reader: An input device, which is able to interpret combinations of marks (bars), which represent data.

Optical Character Recognition (OCR): An input technique base on the process of light scanning stylized characters.

Optical Character Recognition (OCR) device: An input device (a scanner) equipped with a character recognition software. It is used for inputting text documents, and store them in a form suitable for doing word processing of the documents.

Optical Disk: A storage medium, which consists of a rotating disk, which is coated with a thin metal or some other material that is highly reflective. Laser beam technology is used for recording/reading of data on the disk. Also known as laser disks.

Optical Fiber: Hair-thin threads of glass or plastic used as a data transmission medium. They use light signals for data transmission.

Optical Mark Reader (OMR): An input device (a scanner), which is capable of recognizing a pre-specified type of mark made by pencil or pen. Any input data, which is of a choice or selection nature can be recorded for OMR input.

Optical Modem: A synonym for fiber modem.

OS/2: A multitasking operating system with good graphical user interface developed by IBM for PCs.

OSI (Open Systems Interconnection) Network Reference Model: A standard that specifies a conceptual model called the Open Systems Interconnection (OSI) Network Reference Model (OSI Standard 7498), which breaks networked communications into seven layers: Application, Presentation, Session, Transport, Network, Data-Link, and Physical.

OSI Protocol: A communication protocol to interconnect geogra-phically dispersed heterogeneous computers. This protocol has been standardized by the International Standards Organization (ISO).

OSPF (Open Shortest Path First Protocol): A popular protocol used to propagate routing information within a single Autonomous System.

OUI (Organizationally Unique Identifier): A field in an LLC header that specifies which organization assigned the number used for type information.

Output: The result of processing from a device like the computer. It can be still or animated character/picture/graphic/ worksheet, etc. on monitor, sound from speakers, printed paper from the printer, etc.

Output Device: A device used in a computer system to supply information and results of computation to the outside world. Examples are monitor, printer, plotter, screen image projector, and voice response system.

Output Unit: A unit of a computer used to print or display computed results.

Output Unit/Output Devices: A device in a computer system by means of which information is transmitted to the user. Micro films, plotters and printers are hard copy output. Monitors are soft copy output.

Overflow: An overflow is said to occur if the result of an arithmetic operation is larger than the largest number which can be stored in the computer.

P

Packed Decimal Format: A modified form of zoned decimal number, which places two decimal digits into each byte of the field with the exception of the rightmost byte, which contains one digit and the sign of the field.

Packet: A small, self-contained parcel of data sent across a computer network. Each packet contains a header that identifies the sender and recipient, and a payload area that contains the data being sent.

Packet Analyzer: A device used to debug network problems or monitor performance. An analyzer captures packets from a network and reports statistics such as the percentage of broadcast traffic.

Packet Filter: A mechanism in a router used to control traffic, typically as part of an Internet firewall. The packet filter discards all packets that do not adhere to the criteria the manager specifies.

Packet Switching: A data communication method in which the data (message) to be sent is first split up into packets of fixed size each packet is then appended with source and destination addresses, and some control information; and then the packets are sent across the network to their destination. At the receiver end, the packets are reassembled to recreate the message.

Packet Switching Network: Any communication network that accepts and delivers individual packets of information. Most modem networks are packet switching.

Pad: A pad, or key pad, is an array of switches for feeding the data. A digitizer pad is a writing table for feeding writing or lines into the computer.

Paddle: Input device with a joystick. Used while playing TV games.

Page: A programme segment, which is loaded into the main memory only when it is needed for execution.

Page Printer: A high-speed printer with a mechanism, which appears to print an entire page at one time.

Paint: It is a programme which facilitates making free hand drawing with different effects (like rub, spray colours, rotate, etc.) electronically on screen.

Palmtop Computer: A computer with capabilities of a PC which can be accommodated on a person's palm (Size: 16 cm × 12 cm × 5 cm).

PAR (Positive Acknowledgement with Retransmission): The basic technique protocols use to achieve reliable deliver. The receiving protocols returns an acknowledgement when a packet arrives. After transmitting a packet, the sender starts a timer. If the acknowledgement does not arrive before the timer expires, the sender retransmits the packet.

Parallel Adder: An adder in which all the bits of the two operands are added simultaneously.

Parallel Binary Adder: An adder in which all the bits of the two binary numbers are added simultaneously.

Parallel Computers: A set of computers connected together by a high speed communication network and programmed in such a way that they cooperate solve a single large problem.

Parallel Port: Is a jack on the rear side of a computer for placing device for getting signals running in parallel-meaning that a number of signals travel through the port simultaneously (as opposed to serial port, through which the signals travel one after the other).

Parallel Processing: A technology in which a multi-processor system is used to solve complex problems faster by breaking the problem into sub-problems, and allowing different sub-problems to be processed simultaneously by different processors of the multi-processor system.

Parameter: A number, letter or word which can be a value of any variable.

Parity: A way of checking that data have been moved or stored correctly. For odd parity, an extra bit is added to the byte or word to make the resultant total number of '1' bits odd. For even parity, the total is made even.

Parity Bit: An extra bit added to a unit of data, usually each character, to verify that the data is transferred without corruption. A receiver checks the parity on each incoming unit of data. See even parity and odd parity.

Pascal: A high level programming language named after Blaise Pascal. Used for a variety of applications, particularly suitable for non-numeric programming.

Pascal Peripherals: The input/output devices which can be connected to a computer.

Password: A code by which a user gains access to a computer system. It is used for security purposes.

Paste: Cutting out text or image from a file and refixing it in another place.

Patch: A modifications of a software carried out between its two released versions. A patch (modification) is created to fix a newly discovered bug. All the patches are incorporated in a new release version of the software.

Path MTU: The maximum amount of data that can be sent along the path from a source to a destination in one packet. Technically, the path MTU of any network along the path.

Payload: Generically, the data being carried in a packet. The playload of a frame is the data in the frame; the playload of the datagram is the data area of the datagram. See header.

PC (Personal Computer): A small inexpensive self-contained desktop computer intended for an individual user. Most often used for word processing and small database applications.

PCB: Printed Circuit Board A phenolic or glass epoxy board on which electronic components are mounted and interconnected by conducting copper strips bonded to the board.

PCM (Pulse Code Modulation): The technique used to sample audio and encode it for transmission across a telephone network. PCM uses 8000 samples per second, with each sample encoded in 8 bits.

Peer-to-peer: A form of networking in which all computers on the network act as both clients and servers.

Peripheral: Is the term used to describe an input, output or backing storage device, which can be connected to the CPU.

Personal Assistance Software: Software, which enables users to use personal computers for storing and retrieving personal information, and planning and managing personal schedules, contacts, finances, and inventory of important items.

Personal Digital Assistant (PDA): A pocked-sized computer having facilities, such as calendar, calculator, notepad, etc.

PERT (Project Evaluation and Review Technique): A system for planning and progressing time, resource and the cost of projects by linking activities to those which have to precede them.

Petal Printer: Another word for a display-wheel printer.

PGP (Pretty Good Privacy): An encryption technology popular among computer scientists.

Phase Modulation: A form of modulation in which two binary values of digital data are represented by the shift in phase of the carrier signal. That is, a sine wave with phase = 0^0 represents a digital 1, and a sine wave with phase = 180^0 represents a digital 0.

Phase Shift Modulation: A technique modems use to modulate a carrier. The phase of the carrier wave is shifted to encode data.

PHP (PHP: Hypertext Preprocessor): A dynamic Web page technology. Originally named *Perl Helper Pages*, the expansion has been changed to the recursive form listed here. Whenever a PHP page is requested, the Web server invokes the PHP preprocessor to run a script (usually written in Perl) that generates the final form of the page.

Physical Address: Addresses in main memory which are directly addressable and available for storing programme and data.

Physical Layer: The bottom layer of the OSI model where data is transmitted across the actual network medium.

Picosecond: One trillionth of a second.

PIM-DM (Protocol Independent Multicast- Dense Mode): A multicast routing protocol designed to be used across a set of networks that have many listeners (e.g., across Local Area Networks within an organization). See PIM-SM.

PIM-SM (Protocol Independent Multicast-Sparse Model): A multicast routing protocol designed to be used in cases where only a few networks contain listeners (e.g., across Wide Area Networks in the Internet). See PIM-DM.

Ping (Packet Internet Groper): A Net utility that tests Websites.

Ping (Packet Inter-net groper): A programme used to test network connectivity. Ping sends an ICMP Echo Request message to a destination, and reports whether it receives an ICMP Echo Reply as expected.

Pixel: A picture element. It is used to represent one point in a raster-scan display device.

PL/1: A high-level general purpose language.

Plamtop Computer: A battery-operated computer with personal assistance tools. It is small-enough to fit in ones pocket, and operated by keeping it on ones palm.

PLOT: Command in BASIC to show a point on the screen.

<p> HTML tag to begin a new paragraph.

Plotter: An ideal output device, which is often used by architects, engineers, city planners, and others who need to routinely generate high-precision, hard-copy, graphic output of widely varying sizes.

Plug-and-play Networking: Characteristic of any network system that allows a new computer to begin communicating without requiring configuration by the network manager. DHCP provides plug- and play internet connections.

Png (Portable Network Graphics): An extension of picture file.

Point-and-draw Devices: Input devices, which can be used to rapidly point to, and select a particular graphic icon, or menu item from the multiple options displayed on the screen. Many of these devices can also be very effectively used to create graphic elements on the screen, such as lines, curves and freehand shapes. Some of the commonly used point-and-draw devices are mouse, trackball, joystick, electronic pen and touch screen.

Pointer: Another term for cursor.

Point-of-Sale (POS) device: Device An (I/O) device capable of immediately updating sales and inventory records at a central CPU, and producing a printed sales transaction receipt.

Point-to-Multipoint: A mechanism used in an ATM network to deliver a copy of data to multiple destinations. A point-to-multipoint circuit in a connection-oriented network provides functionality equivalent to multicasting in a connectionless network.

Point-to-point: Any network that uses a nonshared technology to connect a pair of systems (e.g., a pair of routers). Point-to-point interconnection is more popular in Wide Area Networks than in Local Area Networks.

Point-to-point Protocol (PPP): A part of the TCP/IP protocol suite, PPP has many options and features, including IP address management and authentication multiplexing and management features, such configuration, testing, error detection, etc. It is commonly used by PCs with modems to dial either the Internet or a corporate network.

Polygon: A closed shape made up of straight lines and having more than two sides.

POP (Post Office Protocol): A protocol that allows a user to access a mailbox (e.g., to read mail messages that have arrived). See SMTP.

Port: Device by which different component in and out of a system unit can be connected.

Portal: A Web "supersite" that offers links to substantial amounts of information and often to other sites; Yahoo is the premiere portal.

Portrait: Orientation of page when printing is widthwise on the page.

Portrait Mode: A mode of printing in which the printed lines are parallel to the shorter edge of the paper.

Positional Number System: A number system in which there are only a few symbols called digits, and these symbols represent different values, depending on the position they occupy in the number. The value of each digit in such a number is determined by the digit itself, the position of the digit in the number, and the base of the number system.

POTS (Plain Old Telephone Service): Conventional analog telephone service.

Power Point: A presentation software used for presenting information in the form of slides.

Pprint: An instruction in BASIC to transmit the output to the Printer.

PPU: Peripheral Processing Unit. A special purpose computer which controls the transfer of information between peripheral devices (disk, tape, printer, etc.) and the main memory of the computer independent of the CPU (same as channel).

Presentation Layer: Layer 6 of the OSI model that translates data into a standard format.

Presentation Slide: A frame in presentation software to show text, pictures, tables, and audio-video background.

Presentation Software: An application software to present our ideas before an audience through slides containing narration, text, picture, graphs, tables, video clippings, etc.

Prestel: British Telecom Viewdata service, with information retrieval and data input on telephone lines.

Preview: (1) A facility to show in advance the changes that happen to a slide when the parameter value is change, given through a dialog box (2) a presentation of a document on the computer screen showing text and graphics with its position and alignment to appear in a printout.

PRI (Primary Rate Interface): An ISDN service that has sufficient bandwidth for larger businesses. See BRI.

Primary Memory: It is the internal storage within computer that stores the unprocessed and processed data as well as the programme instructions. It has limited capacity and is temporary in nature. RAM is primary memory.

Primary Storage: A temporary storage area, which is built into the computer hardware, and in which instructions and data of a programme reside mainly when the programme is being executed by the CPU.

Print: An instruction in BASIC to transmit the output to the Printer.

Print Preview: Gives a view on computer screen how a document/file will appear on paper.

Printer: A device which can print out the information from a computer. Used for computer output. A line printer prints a line of type at a time, a serial printer prints one character at a time.

Private Line: See leased line.

Problem Oriented Languages: High level languages designed to solve a narrow class of special problems. The language does not describe the detailed algorithm to solve the problem but precisely states the problem and its data.

Procedure: A set of instructions to perform a specific task, e.g., procedure for drawing a circle.

Procedure Oriented Language: High level languages with the structure to describe in detail a general class of algorithms.

Process: A programme in execution. Also known as a job.

Processor: The part of the computer where the processing is done. If the processor is on a single chip, it will be called a microprocessor.

Processor Socket: Component in the motherboard to fit processor.

Product Term: The Boolean product of two or more literals equivalent to an AND operation.

Programme: A set of sequenced instructions (written in a language that can be understood by a computer) used to direct and control the operations of the computer to solve a problem, or to perform a particular task.

Programme Control (PC) Register: A register, which holds the address of the next instruction to be executed.

Programme Counter: Also called PC. A register in CPU which stores the address of the next instruction to be carried out by it.

Programme Design Language (PDL): See pseudocode.

Programme Library: A collection of complete programmes, subroutines, and programme modules, which have already been developed, tested, and documented, usually as a result of other programming projects.

Programmable Interconnect Array (PIA): An array consisting of conductors that run throughout the CPLD chip and to which connections from the macrocells in each LAB can be made.

Programmable Read-Only Memory (PROM): Similar to read only memory with the exception that these chips can be reprogrammed by using special external equipment.

Programmer: A fixture into which an SPLD is inserted for programming. The programmer is connected to a computer running HDL software.

Programming: Use of a programming language to convert broad system specification into mechanic instruction.

Programming Language: A set rules or conventions for instructing the computer. A language using machine readable codes and symbols alone is called "low level language" when words or ordinary language are also used along with symbols it is called a "high level language."

PROM: Programmable read-only semiconductor memory; an SPLD with a fixed AND array and programmable OR array; used as a memory device and normally not as a logic circuit device.

Promiscuous Mode: A mode in which a computer connected to a shared network captured all packets, including packets destined for other computers. Promiscuous mode is useful for networking monitoring, but presents a security risk for a production network. Many standard Interfaces allow promiscuous mode.

Propagation Delay: The time required to send a signal across a network. The term comes from electrical engineering terminology and signal propagating down a wire.

Propagation Delay Time: The time interval between the occurrence of an input transition and the occurrence of the corresponding output transition in a logic circuit.

Protocol: A design that specifies the details of how computers interact, including the format of messages they exchange and how errors are handled. See protocol suite.

Protocol Address: A number assigned to a computer that is used as the destination address in packets sent to that computer. Each IP address is 32 bits long; other protocol families use other sizes of protocol addresses.

Protocol Configuration: A step that a computer system must perform to assign values to parameters before protocol software can be used. Usually, protocol configuration requires a system to obtain a protocol address.

Protocol Data Unit (PDU): A unit of data that consists of a header, which is defined by the protocol in use, followed by various application data.

Protocol Port Number: A small integer used to identify a specific application programme on a remote computer. Transport protocol handles a subset of all possible details. The Internet uses the TCP/IP protocol suite. See stack.

Protocol Suite: A set of protocols that work together to provide a seamless communication system. Each protocol handles a subset of all possible details. The internet uses the TCP/IP protocol suite. See stack.

Prototype: An early version of a machine, built to see how well it will work and to experiment with.

Prototypic: The process of developing a small working model of a final operational system to demonstrate the concepts, look, and feel of the final system.

Provisioned: An adjective used to describe a network facility that is configured manually (e.g., a provisioned circuit is established manually). The term derives from the telecommunications industry.

PSET: A instruction in basic to draw a point.

Pseudocode: A programming analysis tool, which is used for planning programme logic. It is an imitation of actual computer instructions written in a natural language, such as English. Also known as Programme Design Language (PDL).

PSK (Phase Shift Keying): Another terminology used for phase modulation. In PSK the phase of a sine wave carrier is 0 or π depending on whether a 0 or a 1 is to be transmitted. In ν PSK, n values of phase of the carrier are used to represent ν strings of bits (0..0 to 1..1).

PSTN (Public Switched Telephone Network): The conventional telephone network, including mechanisms for call setup and accounting.

Public-domain Software : A software, which is available free, or for a nominal charge from the bulletin boards, or user-group libraries on the Internet. Also known as shareware or user-supported software.

Pull-Down Menu: The MENU that is displayed when an item of a major menu is clicked: for eg:-when the menu FILE is clicked, new, open, save and copy are displayed as pull down menu.

Pull-up Resistor: A resistor with one end connected to the dc supply voltage used to keep a given point in a circuit HIGH when in the inactive state.

Pulse: A sudden change from one level to another, followed after a time, called the pulse width, by a sudden change back to the original level.

Pulse Width (t_w): The time interval between the 50 per cent points of the leading and trailing edges of the pulse; the duration of the pulse.

PVC (Permanent Virtual Circuit): A connection from one computer to another through a connection-oriented network. A PVC is permanent in the sense that it survives computer reboots or power cycles; a PVC is virtual because it is achieved by placing routes in routing tables, not by establishing physical wires. ATM expands the acronym to Permanent Virtual Channel. See SVC.

Q

QIC: Quarter-inch cassette; a type of magnetic tape.

QoS (Quality of Service): Term applied to any mechanism that gives statistical guarantees about the service received. QoS mechanisms achieve guarantees by discarding some of the packets from users who do not purchase high-quality service.

Quantization: The process whereby a binary code is assigned to each sampled value during analog-to- digital conversion.

Quarter Inch Cartridge Tapes: Magnetic tape of width 0.25 inch sealed inside a cartridge in which bits are recorded along 9 to 30 serpentine tracks.

Query By Example (QBE): A software tool, which enables database users to specify search criteria by providing a front end for the query language, which collects the facts about a query from the user, and composes query language statements internally.

Query Language: A language, which enables users to define their requirements for extracting the desired information from the database in the form of queries.

Questionnaire: A set of questions used for a survey.

Queuing Delay: The total amount of time a packet must wait in packet switches as it travels through a packet switching network. The queueing delay is related to the amount of traffic in a network—when no other packets are being sent, the queueing delay is zero.

Quotient: The result of a division.

R

Race: A condition in a logic network in which the difference in propagation times through two or more signal paths in the network can produce an erroneous output.

RADIUS (Remote Authentication Dial-In-User Service): A protocol that a computer system uses during bootstrap to obtain an IP address.

Radix: The number of distinct symbols used to represent numbers in a system for enumeration (same as base).

RAID (Redundant Array of Inexpensive Disks): An array of inexpensive disks from which data can be retrieved in parallel from each disk in the array thereby increasing speed of data retrieval. Reliability of data retrieved is improved by storing error detecting bits in addition to the information carrying bits.

RAM: Stands for Random Access Memory. It is the memory which may be read from and written to by the programmer during programme execution. It is a volatile memory.

Random File: See direct file.

Random Number: The numbers which are generated without any order/sequence e.g., throwing a dice.

Random Scan Display: Also known as vector display or calligraphic display. This displays images by breaking them up into points, lines and segments of standard curves. The image is refreshed.

Random/direct-access Storage Device: A storage device in which access to any stored information is direct, and approximately equal access time is required for accessing any information irrespective of its location. Magnetic, optical and magneto-optical disks are typical examples of such a storage device.

Raster File: File to store rater pictures.

Raster Graphics: Graphic objects composed of patterns of dots called pixels.

Raster Image: A picture file making style where colour of each dots in the picture will be saved.

Raster Scan: The generating of images on a screen by focusing an electronic beam on phosphor-coated screen.

Raster Scan Display: In this display the image to be displayed is stored as a matrix of pixels. A pixel is usually several bits, the number of bits depend on whether of the display is a colour or monochrome display. The pixel storage is called a frame buffer or a refresh buffer. As an electron beam scans a CRT from left to right the pixels are retrieved from the frame buffer and used to modulate the beam and display the image.

Read: The process of retrieving data from a memory.

Read-Data: Instruction in BASIC to take out data from a specified address.

Read-Only Memory (ROM): A non-volatile memory chip in which data are stored permanently, and cannot be altered by the programmer.

Real-time Processing: The process in which the system is geared to accept data relating to an activity, to process it and to produce an output immediately.

Real-time System: A system in which a computer is used to control a physical system operating independently. The time taken to compute should match the needs of the physical system.

Reassembly: The procedure a receiver uses to recreate a copy of an original datagram from the fragments that arrive. See fragmentation.

Reboot: To restart the computer. When computer hangs, we restart the computer by rebooting.

Record: A collection of related items of data treated as a unit.

Record Length: A measure of the size of a record, usually specified in units, such as characters.

Recursion: Is a process that occurs when a software procedure calls itself while running.

Recycle: To undergo transition (as in a counter) from the final or terminal state back to the initial state.

Recycle Bin: A folder on the hard disk. When a file is deleted it goes to recycle bin folder from where it can be restored. To permanently delete a file from hard disk one has to further delete it from recycle bin folder.

Redirect: An ICMP error message sent from a router to a host. The message specifies that the host has an incorrect route which should be changed, and specifies the destination and a correct next-hop to reach that destination.

Redirector: A software component in a protocol suite that intercepts requests from applications and determines whether the service is local or remote.

Reduced Instruction Set Computer (RISC) Architecture: An architecture of CPUs with a small instruction set, fixed-length instructions, and reduced references to memory to retrieve operands.

Redundant Array of Inexpensive Disks (RAID): See disk array.

Refresh: To renew the contents of a dynamic memory by recharging the capacitor storage cells.

Refresh Display: A cathode ray tube in which images are to be repetitively displayed 30 to 60 times per second to perceive a stationary image.

Register: A digital circuit capable of storing and shifting binary information; typically used as a temporary storage device.

Registered: A PLD output configuration where the output comes from a flip-flop.

Registers: Small, high-speed storage units, which are used to hold the information on a temporary basis when there is an interpretation and execution of instructions by the CPU. Data stored in a specific register have a special meaning to the CPU.

Relational Database: A database model in which the data elements are organized in the form of multiple tables, and the data in one table is related to data in another table though the use of a common field.

Relay: A switch operated by electricity. Unlike a transistor, a relay has moving parts.

REM (Short for REMARK): A programming statement which is not processed by the computer, but which is used by the programmer to make it clear to the operator what the programme is doing.

Remainder: The amount left over after a division.

Remote Access: Accessing a computer from a distant station using communication facilities.

Remote Login: The facility to login and use a remote computer in a network from a user's terminal.

Repair: To remove a virus from a file and bring the file to its original state, i.e., uninfected file.

Repeater: A hardware device used to strengthen signals being transmitted on a network.

Replay: A condition in which the arrival of a copy of an old packet confuse communication. For example, if a copy of a packet that requests termination of a communication is delayed until after a new communication has begun, the packet can incorrectly cause termination of the new communication. Protocols must be designed to prevent replay from causing problems.

Report File : A file, which holds a copy of a report generated by a data processing application in computer accessible form, until it is convenient to print it.

Report Generator: A software, which enables the users of a database to design the layout of a report, so that it can be presented in the desired format.

Report Programme Generator (RPG): A business oriented, general purpose programming language designed to generate the output reports resulting from the processing of common business applications.

RESET: The state of a flip-flop or latch when the output is 0; the action of producing a RESET state.

Resistor: A component which resists the passage of electricity.

Resize: Changing the size.

Response Time: The elapsed time between submission of a job to the system for processing, and the first response produced by the system for the job.

Restore: To return to normal position, e.g., when a deleted file is restored from recycle bin folder, it comes to its original location.

Retransmission: The retransmission of a packet that has been sent previously. Transport protocols use retransmission to achieve reliability. See PAR.

Reverse Address Resolution Protocol (RARP): A part of the TCP/IP protocol suite that translates a physical address into an IP address.

Reverse Bias: A voltage polarity condition that prevents a *pn* junction of a transistor or diode from conducting current.

RF (Radio Frequency): A range of frequencies used for sending radio signals through the air (e.g., from a commercial radio station). Wireless network technologies use RF.

RF modem: A modem that can send and receive information by modulating a radio frequency carrier. RF modems are used in wireless network technologies.

RFC (Request For Comments): The documents in which standards for TCP/IP protocols are published.

Right Click: Clicking on the right button on the mouse.

RIGHT$: Command in BASIC to select the last letter in a string.

Ring Counter: A register in which a certain pattern of 1s and 0s is continuously recirculated.

Ring Network: A computer network in which there is no host computer for controlling other computers, and each computer in the network has communicating subordinates.

Ring Topology: A network architecture in which computers are linked into a cycle with the first connected to the second, the second connected to the third, and so on until the last connects back to the first. Ring topology is usually used in Local Area Networks.

RIP (Routing Information Protocol): A protocol that uses the dance-vector approach to propagate routing information within an Autonomous System.

Ripple Carry: A method of binary addition in which the output carry from each adder becomes the input carry of the next higher-order adder.

Ripple Counter: An asynchronous counter.

Rise Time: The time required for the positive-going edge of a pulse to go from 10 per cent of its full value to 90 per cent of its full value.

RISK (Reduced Instruction Set Computer): A processor architecture which uses uniform instruction length, simple addressing mode, references to memory only to load and store operands, small number of instructions to simplify control unit design, pipelined instruction execution to enable at least one instruction to be executed in each clock cycle.

RJ-45 (Registered Jack 45): The type of connector used with twisted pair Ethernet.

RJE System: A Remote Job Entry System. A small computer and I/O units located at a geographically remote point connected to another larger computer via a communication channel.

RLE: Run Length Encoding is a method used to compress data to be stored usually on disks.

RMI (Remote Method Invocation): The object-oriented version of remote procedure call. See RPC.

Robot: A machine which can perform some of the movements of a person or animal, or a machine which moves and uses tools according to programmed instructions.

Rogue Value: An artificial value signifying the end of a list of data.

ROM: An abbreviation for Read Only Memory. The programmer cannot write on ROM. The software in the ROM is fixed during manufacturing. However, the user can read (and use for definite purposes) what the software has to offer.

Root Server: A domain name server that knows the locations of top-level domains such as *.com* and *.edu*. See DNS and domain.

Rotation Scaling Tool: Tool in a graphic software to rotate and change dimension of a selected picture.

Route Propagation: The act of passing routing information from one router to another. See EGP and IGP.

Route Server: A server that contains complete routing information for the global Internet. All route servers together form the routing abiter system.

Routed: A UNIX programme that implements the RIP route propagation protocol.

Router: The basic building block of an internet. A router is a computer that attaches to two or more networks and forwards packets according to information found in its routing table. Routers in the Internet run the IP protocol. See host.

Routine: An ordered set of instructions meant for general or frequent use.

Routing: The selection of actual path to be used to transmit a message in a wide-area network environment.

Routing Arbiter System: The system of route servers that each contain complete information about all destinations in the global internet.

Routing Information Protocol (RIP): A part of the TCP/IP protocol suite, RIP establishes communication between routers to share routing information.

Routing Table: A table use by routing software to determine the next hop for a packet. A routing table is kept in a router's memory.

Row: A horizontal array of data.

RPB (Reverse Path Broadcasting): A technique used to prevent broadcast packets from traversing a topological loop.

RPC (Remote Procedure Call): A mechanism used to build clients and servers. RPC inserts code in a programme to allow a procedure call to extend across a network.

RPG: Acronym for Report Programme Generator. A high-level language designed to construct programmes that generate business-oriented printed reports.

RS 232-C Standard: A standard defined by Electronics Industries Association (USA) which specifies the interface between computers, modems and terminals.

RS-232: The technical of the standard used for serial data connections such as those between a keyboard and a computer. The standard defines such details as the voltage used to represent a *1* and a *0.*

RS-232-C Interface: A standard interface used for interconnecting user terminals to computers. It was defined by the Electronics Industrial Association (USA).

RTP (Real-time Transport Protocol): The protocol used with IP telephony to transfer digitized audio (and possibly video). RTP sends a timestamp that allows a receiver to play the stream exactly as it was recorded.

Run: 1. Instruction to carry out a group of instructions or instruction programme in the computers. 2. execute a computer programme.

Run Time: The time required to complete a single, continuous, execution of an object programme.

S

Sampling Theorem: A theorem which states that if an analog signal $s(t)$ has f_h as its highest frequency component, then a little more than $2f_h$ samples of $s(t)$.

Satellite: Something which revolves around something else. Usually, this refers to man-made devices orbiting around the earth, which are often used for communicating or transmitting information.

Save: Process of saving and storing an information or programme in either the hard disk, CD ROM or floppy disc.

Scanner: A light sensitive device that can convert a visual image on paper or other medium into digital signals for a computer.

Schema: The complete logical structure of a database.

Schema Builder: A software tool, which enables a user to define a database schema interactively by prompting the user to enter the field name, field type, field size and so on for each field.

Schottky: A specific type of transistor-transistor logic circuit technology.

Screen: 1. The front of the monitor on which images are displayed. 2. Instruction in BASIC to convert ordinary screen into graphic screen.

Screen Image Projector: An output device, which is used to project information from a computer on to a large screen (such as cloth screen or a wall), so that it can be simultaneously viewed by a large group of people.

Scribe: A person who makes handwritten copies of a document or book.

Scripting Language: Language which has facilities to glue existing application programmes called components to create more complex programmes.

Scroll: The Process of moving information on a computer page from top to bottom and back or to up and down.

Scroll Bar: These are horizontal or vertical rectangular strips, usually appearing at right and bottom side of a window on the screen that enables the user to pan across the screen. Horizontal scroll bar allows us to view widthwise while vertical scroll bar is for lengthwise view.

Scrolling: Using programme-specified ways (by the use of keys or mouse) to move the items displayed in a window up or down, or left or right to see parts of the file that extend past the bottom or top or sides of the window.

SDH (Synchronous Digital Hierarchy): A set of standards developed by telephone companies for high-speed digital circuits.

SDRAM: Synchronous dynamic random-access memory.

Search: To look for a particular character/word in a file or document on the Internet.

Search Engine: Websites that exist to help users find other Websites; Google (www.google.com) is one of the best search engines.

Second Generation Computers: Computers built during the period 1956-65 which used transistors in CPU, magnetic core main memories and high level languages FORTRAN and COBOL for programming.

Secondary Memory/storage: It is backing storage like a floppy. Information stored on it can be retrieved by feeding it into the computer's primary memory via an input device.

Secondary Storage: See auxiliary memory.

Second-generation Computers: Computers built during the period 1955 and 1964. They used transistors in CPU, and magnetic cores for main memory. On software front, they used high-level languages like FORTRAN and COBOL for programming, and batch operating systems.

Sector: The smallest unit with which any disk can work. Disk drives are designed to access only whole sectors at a time.

Secure Proxy: An application gateway that is part of a firewall. A secure proxy allows users on one side of the firewall to access a specific service on the other side of the firewall according to the organization's security policy.

Security: Policies and mechanisms, which deal with protecting the various resources and information of a computer system against destruction and unauthorized access.

Seek Time: In a disk system, the time required for a read/write head to move to the track where the data to be read or written is stored. Maximum seek time equals the time taken for the head to move from the outermost track to the innermost track.

Segment: A single piece of cable that forms a bus network. Multiple segments can be connected by bridges or routers. A hub stimulates a single segment.

Segmentation and Reassembly: The term ATM uses for the division of a large message into small cells for transmission across an ATM network. On the sending computer, the AAL5 protocol segments the message; on the receiving computer, AAL5 reassembles the message.

Select: The process of selecting a particular part or area in the screen using the keyboard or the mouse. There are key board short cuts also for selection.

Selection Logic: A programme construct, which is used for selecting the proper path out of two or more alternative paths in the programme logic. Also known as decision logic.

Self-documenting Languages: Programming languages, which do not require much explanation to be understood by someone reading the programme instruction. For example, COBOL language.

Semantic Error: An error of meaning (a logic error).

Semantic Rule: Rules to assign meanings to valid statements of a language. These rules define what computations are to be carried out for each valid statement.

Semiconductor Storage: A storage device whose storage elements are formed as solid-state electronic components on an integrated circuit chip.

Sensor: A device for sensing something that is happening for reading changes in, for example temperature or light levels.

Sequence Logic: A programme construct, which is used for performing instructions one after another in sequence.

Sequential: Serial, one after another.

Sequential Access: Retrieving data serially starting from the beginning.

Sequential Circuit: A digital circuit whose logic states follow a specified time sequence.

Sequential File: A file in which records are stored one after another in an ascending or descending order determined by the value of the key field of the records.

Sequential Processing: A technique in which a number of similar items or transactions to be processed are grouped together and processed in a designated sequence.

Sequential Storage: Secondary storage where data are stored serially, such as magnetic tape, cassette, paper tape, etc.

Sequential-access Storage Device: A storage device in which information can only be retrieved in the same sequence in which it is stored. Magnetic tape is a typical example of such storage device.

Serial: Having one element following another, as in a serial transfer of bits; occurring, as pulses, in sequence rather than simultaneously.

Serial Access Memory: A memory from which information is retrieved sequentially one bit after another.

Serial Adder: An adder in which the bits of the operands are added on after another.

Serial Line: A physical wire between two points over which data is sent one bit at a time. RS 232-C is often used with serial lines.

Serial Port: A device by which the computer can transfer data to an attached instrument and back.

Server: When two programmes communicate over a network, a client is the one that initiates communication, while a server is the programme that waits to be contacted a given programme can act as a server for one service and a client for another.

Server Computer: In a client-server computing environment, a computer, which manages a shared resource and provides a set of shared user services to the clients. It runs the server process, which services client requests for use of the resource managed by the server.

Session Cookie: A cookie that a browser holds in memory. Because it is kept in memory instead of on disk, a session cookie only persists while the browser is running.

Session Layer: Layer 5 of the OSI model that establishes, maintains, and terminates sessions across the network. This layer manages name recognition, synchronization, and some access features, such as when a device can transmit and how long it can transmit.

SET: The state of a flip-flop or latch when the output is 1; the action of producing a SET state.

Set-up Time: The time interval required for the control levels to be on the inputs to a digital circuit, such a flip-flop, prior to the triggering edge of clock pulse.

Shannon's Theorem: An important result that specifies the maximum data rate that can be achieved over a transmission channel that has noise associated with it. See Nyquist's Interesymbol Interference Theorem.

Shareware: See public-domain software.

Shielded Twisted Pair: A cable that contains one (or more) twisted pairs of wire surrounded by a heavy metal shield similar to the shield that surrounds a single wire in a coaxial cable. The shield protects the inner pairs of wires from electrical interference.

Shift: To move binary data from stage to stage within a shift register or other storage device or to move binary data into or out of the device.

Shift Key: A key on a typewriter used to adjust the action of the machine so that it types capital letters.

Short Cut: A shorter method to carry out certain commands instead of going through the menu.

Shortcuts: Substitute of a key combination that can be clicked to do a particular task.

Shut Down: To stop the working of the computer and disconnect supply.

Sign Bit: The left-most bit of the binary number that designates whether the number is positive (0) or negative (1).

Signal Loss: The amount of electrical energy lost as a wave travels down a medium such as a copper wire. A network connection cannot be arbitrarily long because the signal loss eventually makes the wave too weak to detect.

Signaling: A telephone company term for the mechanism that provide call setup and termination.

Silicon: The material which provides the base for solid state microelectronic component. It is purified sand. It is the raw material on integrated circuits.

Silicon Chip: See Chip.

Silicon Valley: A group of cities in South California USA, where most of the electronic components manufacturing firms are situated, engaged in the manufacture of computers.

SIMM: Single-in-line memory module.

Simple Network Management Protocol (SNMP): A part of the TCP/IP protocol suite, SNMP monitors remote hosts over a TCP/IP network.

Simplex: A data transmission mode in which data can flow only in one direction.

Simulation: The imitation of certain behaviour of a system, or of some aspects of that behaviour, by another system. The imitation may be in the form of a model that can be manipulated by a computer or a device under the control of a computer to achieve the imitation.

Single Address Computer: A computer in which a machine instruction specifies only one operand address.

Single In-line Memory Module (SIMM): A memory board with memory chips on it. Memory chips can be added on the board to increase the computer's main memory capacity.

SIP (Session Initiation Protocol): A protocol developed by the IETF that provides signaling for IP telephony systems.

Slash Notation: A syntactic form used in CIDR addressing and routing. An address is given in dotted decimal followed by a slash and an integer between 0 and 32 that represents the length of the address mask.

Slide Rule: A mechanical calculating device using the same principles as logarithm tables.

Sliding Window: A technique that a protocol can use to improve throughput by allowing a sender to transmit additional packets before receiving any acknowledgement. A receiver tells a sender how many packets can be sent at one time (called a window size).

Slot: Location in a system unit to connect cards.

Small Scale Integration (SSI): A measure of circuit density of a chip. Measured generally in tens of gates.

Smart Card: An Electronic card having a built-in microprocessor chip. Data to be encoded on the card is permanently stored in the memory of the chip.

Smart Terminal: A terminal having local data editing capability, and the ability to consolidate input data, before sending them to the main computer. It has a microprocessor, some internal storage, and I/O capabilities.

SMDS (Switched Multi-megabit Data Service): A connectionless Wide Area Network technology offered by telephone companies.

SMPS (Switched Mode Power Supply): The part of a system unit which distributes power supply to all segments of a computer.

SMT: Surface-mount technology; an IC package technique in which the packages are smaller than DIPs and are mounted on the printed surface of the PC board.

SMTP (Simple Mail Transfer Protocol): The protocol used to transfer e-mail from one computer to another across the Internet. SMTP is part of the TCP/IP protocol suite. See POP.

SNAP (SubNetwork Attachment Point): Part of IEEE LLC/SNAP header used to identify the type of a packet. The entire header is 8 octets, with the SNAP portion occupying the last five. See LLC.

Sniffer: A synonym for network analyzer taken from a popular product.

SNMP (Simple Network Management Protocol): The protocol that specifies how a network management station communicates with agent software in remote devices such as routers; the current version is number 3. SNMP defines the format of messages and their meaning. See MIB.

SOAP (Simple Object Access Protocol): An object-oriented middleware technology.

Socket: Device by which a component can be attached with a computer.

Socket API: A set of procedure that an application programme can use to communicate across a network. The name arise because the set include a socket procedure that must be called to establish communication. See API.

Soft-copy Output: A computer output, which is temporary in nature, and vanishes after use. For example, output displayed on a terminal screen, or spoken out by a voice response system.

Software: The set of instructions that tells the hardware to do something with the data. Software is not a physical component. MS Word and Paint are example of software.

Software Interrupt: An instruction that invokes an interrupt service routine.

Software Package: A group of programmes, which solve a specific problem, or perform a specific type of job. For example, a word-processing package.

Software Piracy: The illegal copying or use of software.

Software: A series of detailed instructions used to direct the operations of input, processing, output and storage in a computer.

SOHO Router (Small Office/Home Office router): An inexpensive IP route that has sufficient capacity for a residence or small office.

Solid State: Electronic components, whose operation depends on the control of electric or magnetic phenomena in solids, such as transistors and diodes.

SONET (Synchronous Optical Network): A standard for digital encoding used by the telephone companies.

Sort: Arrange information alphabetically or in a suitable sequence.

Sorting: Arrangement of letters and words in word processor.

Sound: A command in BASIC to produce a sound in the frequency specified.

Sound Card: An electronic circuit card which can convert the data from computer on sound waves to pan it to speakers.

Source: A sending device of a bus; one of the terminals of a field-effect transistor.

Source Address: An address in a packet that specifies the computer that sent the packet. In a hardware frame, the source address must be a hardware address. In an IP datagram, the source address must be an IP address.

Source Programme: A programme written in a symbolic or high-level language, such as assembly language, COBOL, BASIC, etc.

Space Bar: The key used to insert space equivalent to the size of one letter.

Spam: Unwanted, unsolicited commercial e-mail.

Speaker: Hardware connected to the computer to noise, speech or music output.

Special Character: A graphic character, which is neither a letter, a digit, nor a space character. For example, the dollar sign, comma, period, etc.

Special Purpose Computer: A computer, which is meant for doing only a particular type of jobs.

Speech Out Unit: A unit which will accept strings of ASCII bytes and convert them into spoken words or sentences.

Speech Synthesizer: A digital device that can create speech on instruments from a computer. It can literally talk back to the operator but the user can talk to the computer in a limited manner only.

Speed-power Product: A performance parameter that is the product of the propagation delay time and the power dissipation in a digital circuit.

Spell Check: The process of examining a word for correct spelling. It is inbuilt facility in a word processing programme which offers possible corrections when it finds word which it does not recognize.

SPF (Shortest Path First): A general link-status algorithm that routers can use compute routes. See distance-vector and link-status.

Spider: Spiders (also known as crawlers) search the Web for information; search engines use spiders to find Web pages.

SPLD: Simple programmable logic device; an array of AND gates and OR gates that can be programmed to achieve specified logic functions. Four types are FROM, PLA, and GAL.

Spread Spectrum: A transmission technique used to avoid interference and achieve higher throughput. Instead of a single carrier frequency, a sender and receiver agree to use a set of frequencies, either at the same time or by changing from one to another. The technique is especially important for wireless networks.

Spreadsheet: A programme that manipulates data in the cells of a table and displays them on the screen. The cells contains numerical data and formulae, or text or date, etc. A spreadsheet can be used for 'what-if' analysis and many other applications involving tables of numbers with independent rows and columns. It is commonly used as a general purpose simulation tool.

SQL: A standard query language for relational databases.

S-R Flip-flop: A SET-RESET flip-flop.

SRAM: Static random-access memory; a type of volatile read/write semiconductor memory.

SS7 (Signalling System 7): The standard for signaling (i.e., call setup and termination) used in the PSTN.

Ssh (Secure Shell): An application-layer technology that allows remote login. Ssh is similar to TELNET except that ssh uses encryption to guarantee confidentiality.

SSI: Small-scale integration; a level of fixed-function IC complexity in which there are twelve fewer equivalent gates per chip.

SSL (Secure Sockets Layer): An encryption technology that provides confidentiality for data sent over a TCP connection. SSL is used with Web transfers that involve commerce (e.g., sending a credit card number).

Stack: A memory in which information, which is stored last is on top, and is retrieved first. Also known as LIFO (Last-in-first-out) storage.

Stage: One storage element (flip-flop) in a register.

Stand-alone: In a distributed data processing system, it refers to a computer system, which has an independent (from a central-site computer) processing and storage capability.

Star Network: A network in which multiple computes are connected to a central host computer. These computers are not linked directly to each other, and can communicate only via the host computer.

Star Topology: A network architecture that consists of a central hub to which all computers connect. Star topologies are often used with Local Area Networks (e.g., twisted pair Ethernet). See hub and switch.

State Diagram: A graphic depiction of a sequence of states or values.

State Machine: A logic system exhibiting a sequence of states conditioned by internal logic and external inputs; any sequential circuit exhibiting a specified sequence of states.

Stateful Server: A server that is designed so the action performed for a given request depends on the prior history of requests. See stateless server.

Stateless Server: A server that handles each request independently. Most servers are designed to be as stateless as possible. See stateful server.

Statement: In programming, an expression or generalized instruction in a source language.

Statement Number: Number given to lines of commands in languages like BASIC.

Static Document: A page of information available on the World Wide Web. The contents of a static document do not change until the author places new information in the document. See active document, dynamic document, and URL.

Static Memory: A volatile conductor memory that uses flip-flops as a storage cells and is capable of retaining data without refreshing.

Statistical Multiplexing: A variant of STDM that only services a given source when the source has something to send. The chief advantage of statistical multiplexing arises because it never leaves the communication channel idle while a source has something to send.

Statistician: Somebody who calculates and classifies table of figures.

Status Bar: Information about current command or status of cursor, etc. are displayed on status bar which is normally at the bottom of a window.

STDM (Synchronous Time Division Multiplexing): Any time-division multiplexing mechanism that proceeds round-robin among all sources. The acronym is also expanded to *Slotted Time Division Multiplexing.*

Storage: Areas internal or external to the central processor in which data and programmes can be stored.

Storage Capacity: The amount of data that can be stored on a storage device or main memory.

Storage Hierarchy: A hierarchy of storage technologies (such as cache memory, main memory, secondary storage and mass storage) used in a computer system. This is usually done because a single type of storage is not superior in speed of access, capacity, and cost.

Store and Forward: Characteristic of network that uses packet switches to forward packets. The name arises because each switch along a path to the destination receives a packet and temporarily stores the packet in memory. Meanwhile the switch continuously selects a packet from the queue in memory, routes the packet, and then transmits the packet to the appropriate next hop.

Store and Forward System: A system of computer and/or digital equipment in which messages or signals are sent to a central computer which receives and stores them and forwards them to the specified destinations.

Stored Programme Computer: A computer where the programme to solve a problem, and the necessary data are stored in its memory.

Storyboard: Design of a presentation prepared before its preparation.

String: A series of characters-like a word or a sentence which is processed by a computer.

String Function: Functions used handle strings in programming languages.

Strobing: A process of using a pulse to sample the occurrence of an event at a specified time in relation to the event.

Structured Design: A system design approach in which a difficult problem is broken into smaller problems, which is small enough to manage, but independent enough to solve separately.

Structured Programming: An organized approach to programming involving the use of the three basic control structures-sequence, selection, and iteration, and the use of top-down concepts to decompose main functions into lower level components for modular coding purposes.

STS (Synchronous Transport Signal): A set of standard adopted by common carries for high-speed digital circuits. STS-1 operates at 51.840 Mbps; STS-*n* runs at *n* times that bit rate. See OC.

Study Phase: A system life-cycle phase during which a problem is identified, alternative solutions are studied, and the most feasible solutions is selected.

Style: Technique by which the character of a page, paragraph or letters are totally controlled.

Subfolder: Folder within a folder.

Subnet: A segment of a network.

Subnet Addressing: An extension of the original IP addressing scheme in which an organization uses a single IP prefix for multiple physical networks. See address mask.

Subnet Mask: A synonym for address mask.

Subprocedure: See subroutine.

Subprogramme: See subroutine.

Subroutine: A standardardized programme written in a manner that it can be used as part of another programme whenever necessary. A subroutine is normally invoked through other programmes by the use of CALL statements. Also known as sub-programme and sub-procedure.

Subtracter: A logic circuit used to subtract two binary members.

Subtrahend: The number that is being subtracted from the minuend.

Suite: See protocol suite.

Sum: The result when two or more numbers are added together.

Sum Term: The Boolean sum of two or more literals equivalent to an OR operation.

Sum-of-products (SOP): A form of Boolean expression that is basically the ORing of ANDed terms.

Supercomputers: They are the fastest computers available at any given time and are normally used to solve problems requiring intensive numerical computation.

Superscalar Processor Architecture: A processor architecture in which multiple instructions are executed in one clock cycle.

Surf: To search information on the Internet.

SVC (Switched Virtual Circuit): A connection from one computer to another through a connection-oriented network. An SVC is virtual because it is achieved by placing routes in routing tables, not by establishing physical wires an SVC is switched because it can be created on demand analogous to a telephone call. ATM expands the acronym to Switched Virtual Channel. See PVC.

2-3 Swap: A reference to a cable in which the wire used to receive on the other, and vice-versa. The numbers 2 and 3 refer to the transmit and receive pins on a DB-25 connector.

Swapping: Strong programmes on disk, and then transferring these programmes into main storage as and when they are needed. The technique is used to process large programmes, or several programmes with limited memory.

Switch: An electronic device that forms the center of a star topology network. A switch uses the destination address in a frame to determine which computer should receive the frame.

Switched Network: Any network that uses switches instead of routers. Usually, switching implies connection-oriented technology. ATM is an example of technology that uses switching.

Switching: A general term used to describe the operation of a switch. Because it is associated with hardware, switching is usually higher speed than routing. Also, switching differs from routing because switching uses the hardware address in a frame.

Symbol Table: A table used by a programming language compiler to allocate memory to store variables.

Symbolic Language: See assembly language.

Symbolic Programme: See assembly programme.

SYN (SYNchronization Segment): The initial segment of a TCP transmission. Each side sends a SYN to start a connection. A well-known security attack involves sending a flood of SYN segments.

Synchronous: Characteristic of any communication system in which the sender must coordinate (i.e., synchronize) with the receiver before sending data. Synchronization is usually handled by having the sending hardware transmit regular pulses when no data is available. The receiver uses the pulse to extract data from the incoming signal see asynchronous.

Synchronous: Having a fixed time relationship; occurring at the same time.

Synchronous Communication: Data transmission mode in which the sender and receiver must synchronize with each other to get ready for data transmission, before it takes place.

Synchronous Counter: A type of counter in which each stage is clocked by the same pulse.

Syntax: A set of rules of a programming language, which define the pattern or structure of the word order and punctuation of an instruction. It is analoguous to rules of grammar in English language.

Syntax Error: An error in the use of language construction.

Syntax Errors: Errors in computer programmes, which typically involve incorrect punctuation, incorrect word sequence, undefined terms, or misuse of terms. These errors are automatically detected, and pointed out by language processors.

Syntax Rules: Rules which specify how valid syntactic elements of a programming language can be combined into legal statements of the language.

System: A group of integrated parts (people, methods, machines and materials), which have a common purpose of achieving some objective(s).

System Analysis: A detailed step-by-step investigation of related procedures to see what must be done, and the best way of doing it.

System Analyst: The individual responsible for planning a computer data processing system. He/she utilizes tools, such as flowcharts, decision tables, programme design language, etc. These plans are then passed to the computer programmer.

System Commands: Commands used to communicate with the operating system of the computer.

System Files: The files that make up the operating system.

System Programmer: A programmer who prepares system software.

System Programmes: The programmes which enables the hardware to function.

System Software: A set of one or more programmes designed to control the operation, and extend the processing capability of a computer system.

System Unit: The main part of a computer which stores and processes data.

T

T1, T3: The designations that telephone companies use for popular point-to-point digital circuits. A T1 circuit operates at 1.544 Mbps; a T3 circuit operates at 44.736 Mbps. See DS-0, DS-1, DS-3.

Tab: (1) Facility to move the curser at prefixed small distance between words, to prepare small tables, (2) The space given between two words using the tab key (3) Mechanism in dialogue boxes like paragraph in word processors to organize more than one information in the same box.

Table: A way of presentation of data in rows and columns.

Tag: The mechanism in HTML to command various features.

Tail-end Modem: A modem located at a customer's site (e.g., residence). See head-end modem.

Tapc Density: The amount of data, which can be placed over a given length of tape, the density is usually expressed in bytes or characters per inch.

Tape Drive: A device used for storage and retrieval of data stored on magnetic tape medium.

Task Bar: The horizontal bar seen at the bottom of a Window. Start button, time, etc. are displayed on the task bar.

TCP (Transmission Control Protocol): The TCP/IP protocol that provides application programmes with access to a connection-oriented communication service. TCP offers reliable, flow-controlled delivery. More important TCP accommodates changing conditions in the internet by adapting its retransmissions scheme. See UDP.

TCP Splicing: A technique related to NAT that uses segment mapping to join two separate TCP connections.

TCP/IP: The protocol suite used in the Internet. Although the suite contains many protocols, TCP and IP are two of the most important.

TDM (Time Division Multiplexing): Characteristic of a mechanism that allows multiple senders to share a communication medium by taking turns. At any time, only one sender transmits across the channel. See FDM>

Telecommunications: Transmission of data between computer system and/or terminals at different locations through telephone facilities.

Telematique: A French term for computing and telecommunication.

Teletax: A standard for transmission of electronic mail.

Teletex: The system linking T.V. and telephone systems so that you dial up information on the telephone and read it on the television screen.

Teletext: A video text that broadcasts to receiving devices. Several pages of written papers broadcasted to general consumers or. television. (All important informations for use in a cosmopolitan city, like railway/air timings, important spot news, currency exchange rates, information on income tax, details of conferences and important events etc. are kept on being broadcast throughout the day.

Teletype (Teletypewriter): A terminal with keyboard input and printed output, and sometimes with paper tape input and output also.

Telnet: An application level protocol, which allows a user to log in to another computer from his/her current computer in a network environment.

Template: A predesigned document; a Web page template, for instance, requires the user simply to fill in some blanks to produce a publishable document.

Tera: Used to represent $1024 \times 1024 \times 1024 \times 1024 = 2^{40} \approx 10^{15}$. abbreviated form T.

Terabytes (TB): Memory storage equal to about one trillion (10^{12}) bytes.

Teraflop: 10^{12} floating-point arithmetic operations per second.

Term Sheet Commitment: A written offer from a venture capitalist that sets out how much money the firm will put into a start-up in return for what percentage of ownership.

Terminal: A device, often consisting of keyboard and/or visual display unit that is connected to a computer and can be used for the remote entry and receipt of information.

Terminal Count: The final state in a counter's sequence.

Terminator: A device attached to the end of a wire or a transmission cable to prevent electrical signals from reflecting back. A bus network such as an Ethernet requires each end of the cable to have a terminator.

Testing: The process of making sure that the programme performs the intended task.

Text Box: A box shaped facility to type text matte.

TFTP (Triviali File Transfer Protocol): A protocol used to transfer a file from one computer to another. TFTP is simpler than FTP, but does not have as much capability.

THEN: Help us to do the next action, if the 'IF' rule in BASIC is correct.

Then: IF : A statement is basic which specifies the operations to be carried out when the conditions following 'IF' is satisfied.

Thermal Printer: A printer device, which utilizes paper that is sensitive to heat.

Thermal Printing: Printing using heat-sensitive paper.

Thick Wire Ethernet: An informal term used for the original DIX Ethernet.

Thicknet: A synonym for thick wire Ethernet.

Thin Wire Ethernet: An informal term used for the version of Ethernet that uses thinner coaxial cable.

Thinnet: A synonym for thin wire Ethernet.

Third-generation Computers: Computers built between 1964 and 1975, which used integrated circuits in CPU, high speed magnetic core main memories, powerful high-level languages, and time sharing operating system.

Throughput: The total amount of useful processing carried out by a computer system within a given time period. It is measured as the number of processes, which are completed by the system per unit time.

Ticker Tape: Paper ribbon used for printing telegraphed messages.

TIFF: Short for 'Tagged Image File Format' A file format for storing images. Usually used for images which are printed.

Time Division Multiplexing: A method of sharing a communication channel in which the total time available in the channel in which the total time available in the channel is allotted a time slice during which he/she may transmit a message. The channel capacity is fully utilized by interleaving a number of data streams belonging to different users into one data stream.

Time Log: A log documentation automatically maintained by many computer systems, which describes in detail how the computer system was used during the day.

Time Sharing System: A computer system designed to allow many users to simultaneously use it.

Time Slice: The short period of time during which a user process gets the attention of the CPU in a time-sharing system. Also known as time slot or quantum.

Time Slot : See time slice.

Timesharing: A mode of computer operation where computer facilities are shared by several users via terminals for different purposes at a same time. The computer actually serves each user serially, but the high speed of the computer makes it appear that the user programmes are all handled simultaneously.

Timing Diagram: A graph of digital waveforms showing the proper time relationship of all the waveforms and how each waveform changes in relation to the others.

Title Bar: The horizontal bar at the top of the screen which displays the name of file along with the name of software on the left and on the right side shows buttons to minimize, restore/ maximize and close the window.

TLD (Top-Level Domain): Any of the domain such as *.com*, *.edu*, or *.org* that form the top level of the domain hierarchy.

Toggle: The action of a flip-flop when it changes state on each clock pulse.

Token Passing: A technique used in ring topology networks to control transmission.

Token Ring: A ring topology network that uses token passing for access control. The phrase also applies to an older token passing ring topology defined by IBM corporation.

Toolbar: A bar which shows the facilities available in a software along with a representative graphic.

Top Down Design: A system design which starts with general concepts and then moves to specifies.

Top-Down Approach: A disciplined approach to system design or programme design in which top-level functions are decomposed into a hierarchy of understandable lower-level modules for better management and easy handling.

Topology: A term used to describe the general shape of a network. Common topologies include bus, point-to-point, ring, and star.

Totem-pole: A type of output in TTL circuits.

Touch Panel: A locator device used in laptop computers as a replacement for a mouse. It is operated by moving a finger over a capcitively coupled glass panel to point to a location on the screen.

Touch Screen: A simple, intuitive, and easy to learn input device, which enables the users to choose from available options by simply touching with their finger the desired icon or menu item displayed on the computer's screen.

TP Ethernet (Twisted Pair Ethernet): See 10BaseT.

Traceroute: A network diagnostic programme that finds the address of all routers between the user's computer and a specified destination. Traceroute sends datagrams with successively larger time-to-live values, and uses ICMP error messages to determine routers along the path.

Tracert: The name that Microsoft uses for the traceroute programme included with its operating systems.

Track: In case of magnetic disk, one of many circular concentric rings used for storing data. In case of magnetic tape, a horizontal strip, or channel, running the full length of the tape, and used for recording data.

Trackball: An input device, which serves as an effective point device.

Trailing Edge: The second transition of a pulse.

Transaction File: A file in which current data are stored for subsequent processing usually in combination with a master file.

Transceiver: An electronic device that connects the Network Interface Card in a computer to a physical medium. Transceivers are used with thick wire Ethernet.

Transducer: A device capable of changing signals from analog form to digital form, or vice-versa.

Transistor: A controlled electronic switch fabricated using a semiconductor. It is extensively used in the design of various electronic equipment.

Transmission Control Protocol/Internet Protocol (TCP/IP): The most widely used protocol suite in the world, and the standard for communication on the Internet.

Transmission Error: Any change introduced as data passes across a network. Transmission errors can be caused by electrical interference or hardware that malfunctions.

Transponder: A device mounted on a communication satellite, which receives, amplifies and retransmits signals from earth stations.

Transport Layer: Layer 4 of the OSI model that prepares data for transmission across the network.

Trap: An interrupt signal sent to CPU by an event within a computer such as hardware error, arithmetic overflow, etc.

Trash: In GNU/Linux operating system the space for storing unused files and folders.

Trigger: A pulse used to initiate a change in the state of a logic circuit.

Tristate: A type of output in logic circuits that exhibits three states: HIGH, LOW and high-Z; also known as 3-state.

Tristate Output Buffer: A logic circuit having three output states: HIGH, LOW and high-impedance (open).

Truncated: Shortened.

Truncated Sequence: A sequence that does not include all of the possible states of a counter.

Trunk Circuit: A term with more than one meaning. Telephone companies use the term to refer to large-capacity circuits that form the main interconnect of the telephone network (e.g., between cities). Cable television companies use the term to refer to the high-capacity coaxial cables used to connect the cable company and neighbourhood concentration points; a trunk circuit can be up to fifteen miles long. See feeder circuit.

Truth Table: A table, which gives the output values for the varies input combinations in case of a logical expression.

TSSOP: Thin shrink small-outline package.

TTL (Time to Live): A value found in the header of an IP datagram. Each router decrements in TTL value. If the TTL reaches zero, the router discards the datagram and send an ICMP error message to the source.

Tunnel: Any mechanism that encapsulates a packet in a high-level protocol for transmission. See IP tunnel and IP in – IP.

Tuple: A group of related fields (a row of a table) in a relational databases.

Turnaround Time: The elapsed time between the submission of job to a computer system for processing, and the completion of the job.

Turnkey Solution: See end-to-end solution.

TV Tuner Card: An electronic circuit by which TV programmes can be watched in a computer.

<Table> HTML tag to show data in table.

.tar.gz AN extension part in the name of a compressed file.

<td> HTML tag commanding the start of a new row.

.tif (Targeted Image File Format): An extension of a picture file.

<title> HTML tag directing the title of a browswer.

<tr> HTML tag to begin a new row in a table.

Twisted Pair: A form of wiring in which a pair of wires is wrapped around one another again and gain. Twisting two wires reduces their susceptibility to electrical interference.

Twisted-pair Cable: A simple inexpensive, and slow wired transmission medium.

U

UDDI (Universal Discovery Description and Integration): A directory service used with middleware.

ULSI: Ultra large-scale integration; a level of IC complexity in which there are more than 100,000 equivalent gates per chip.

Ultra Large Scale Integration (ULSI): Integration of about ten million electronic components on to a single chip.

Ultra Violet EPROM (UVEPROM): An EPROM hip in which the stored information is erased by exposing the chip for some time to ultraviolet light.

Unbundled: A term, which means that the application software is priced separately from the computer hardware.

Unconditional Transfer: A programme instruction, which causes the programme control to flow out of normal sequence conditionally.

Underflow: Condition occurs when the result of an arithmetic operation is smaller than the smallest number which can be stored in the computer.

Undo: Cancellation of the most recent action. It puts the user back to where he has before.

Unibus: A single bus which interconnects I/O units, CPU and memory of a computer.

Unicast: A form of packet delivery in which each computer is assigned a unique address. When a packet is sent to unicast address, exactly one copy of the packet is delivered to the computer to which the address corresponds. Unicast delivery is the most common type. See broadcast, cluster and multicast.

Uniform Resource Locator (URL): An addressing scheme used by WWW browsers to locate sites on the Internet.

Uninterrupted Power Supply (UPS): A batter-supported power unit between an external power source and a computer system, which supplies clean and continuous power even during power failures.

Unit Load: A measure of fan-out. One gate input represents a unit load to the output of a gate within the same IC family.

Universal Gate: Either a NAND gate or a NOR gate. The term universal refers to the property of a gate that permits any logic function to be implemented by that gate or by a combination of gates of that kind.

Universal Product Code (UPC): A universal or standardized optical bar code, which normally appears on retail packages, and which is read by a laser beam scanner.

Universal Shift Register : A register that has both serial and parallel input and output capability.

Unix: A multi-user, time-sharing operating system. It is a very popular operating system, and can be used on a wide variety of computers, ranging from notebook computers to super computers.

UNIX: An operating system designed by AT & T Bell Telephone Laboratories (USA). It is a time sharing O.S. written in C.

Unix Kernel: The inner most core of Unix OS which performs various primitive operations requested by user processes.

Unix Pipe: A facility available in Unix to feed a stream of bytes which are output of a programme as input to another programme.

Unix Shell: A command interpreter supported by the Unix operating system.

Unzipping: See decompression.

Up/down Counter: A counter that can progress in either direction through a certain sequence.

Uplink: A form of packet delivery in which each computer is assigned a unique address. When a packet is sent to a unicast address, exactly one copy of the packet is delivered to the computer to which the address corresponds. Unicast delivery is the most common type. See broadcast, cluster, and multicast.

Uploading: Moving a file from ones own computer to a remote computer in a network environment.

Upstream: The path of data from a residential customer to the Internet. The term is often used with DSL or cable modem technologies. See downstream.

Uptime: The time duration when the computer system is in operation.

Upward Compatible: The ability of hardware or software to function with all of the same equipment and software with which its predecessors could function.

URL (Uniform Resource Locator): A syntactic form used to identify a page of information on the World Wide Web.

USB Port (Universal Serial Bus Port): A way by which external equipments can be attached to a computer.

Usenet: A service on the Internet, which allows a group of Internet users to exchange their views/ideas/information on some common topic, which is of interest to all the members belonging to the group.

User Authentication: Deals with the problem of verifying the identity of a user (person or programme), before permitting access to the requested resource.

User-friendly: A programme or computer system designed in a manner that even individuals who lack computer experience can easily use the system without much training.

User-programmed ROM: A PROM in which the user can load and store "read-only" programmes and data.

User-supported Software : See public-domain software.

Utilities: A set of programmes, which help users in performing system maintenance and other tasks of routine nature.

Utility: A common name used to represent certain small applications like calculator, player etc.

UTP (Unshielded Twisted Pair): Wiring in which pairs of wires are twisted together to minimize interference, but no other shielding is provided. See coaxial cable and shielded twisted pair.

UV EPROM: Ultraviolet erasable programmable ROM.

V

Vacuum tube: The American word for an electronic valve.

Value Added Network (VAN): Enhanced data transmission service provided by doing value addition to the standard services of the common carriers. Added value may include features, such as electronic mail, data encryption/decryption, access to commercial databases, and code conversion for communication between incompatible computers.

Valve: An electronic valve or thermionic valve is a vacuum-filled glass tube which can be used as an amplifier or as a switch.

Variable: A number or character which is stored in a slot in the computer's memory, but which can change or vary at different times.

Variable name: In a programme, the name assigned to a data field, which can assume any of a given set of values.

VBR (Variable Bit Rate): The service used by ATM to transfer data for which the data rate changes over time.

VC (Virtual Circuit): A connection from one computer to another through a connection-oriented network. The term virtual arises because the circuit is achieved by placing routes in routing tables, not by establishing physical wires. Also called a virtual channel.

VDU: A Video Display Unit. An I/O device which consists of a television tube for presenting outputs and a keyboard for entering inputs.

Vector File: A file stored with vector graphics or pictures.

Vector Graphics: Graphic objects composed of patterns of lines, points, circles, arcs, and other geometric shares (vectors), which can be easily represented by few geometric parameters.

Vector Image: Picture file madeup of geometric shapes like circuits, rectangles, ovals etc.

Vector-distance: The original name for distance-vector.

Venture Capitalist (VC): A professional lender of money—often raised from university endowment funds—who seeks out high-potential tech start-ups to fund.

Very Large Scale Integration (VLSI): An electronic circuit with about 10,000 transistors fabricated in a single silicon chip.

Very Small Aperture Terminals (VSATs): Smaller disk antennas having lower power transmitters and receivers, which can be installed at users' sites. It enables a large number of users to benefit from satellite communication.

Video Conferencing: A system in which persons sitting at CRT screens see and talk to each other via a computer-communications network. It saves travelling cost and the valuable time of executives.

Video Display Terminal (VDT): A monitor and a keyboard used together as both an input and an output device. Also known as terminal.

Videotex: Transmission and presentation of text and graphics.

Viewdata: Information retrieval system using domestic television receivers as terminals.

Virtual Channel: A synonym for virtual circuit. The term virtual channel is used with technologies such as ATM. See VC.

Virtual Machine: The concept of adding the operating system layer on top of the bare hardware to manage all parts of the system, and present the users with an interface, which is easier to programme and use.

Virtual Memory: A memory management scheme, which allows an execution of processes, which might not be completely loaded in the main memory. The three basic concepts used for the realization of virtual memory are on-line secondary storage, swapping and demand paging.

Virus: A computer virus is a piece of code attached to a legitimate programme, which, when executed, infects other programmes in the system by replicating and attaching itself to them. In addition to this replicating effect, a virus normally does some other damage to the system, such as corrupting/erasing files.

Virus Scan: Systematic search for detection of any virus in the file with an antivirus programme like Nortron, PC-Cillin, etc.

Vision Input System: An input device, which allows a computer to accept input by seeing an object. The input data in this case is normally an object's shape and features in the form of an image.

Visual Display Unit (VDU): A TV like screen on which information from the computer can be displayed. Similar to a television screen on which text or diagrams can be displayed as output from a computer.

Visualization: Deals with exploring data and information graphically for better comprehension.

VLSI: Very Large Scale Integrated circuit. An electronic circuit with about 100,000 transistors fabricated in a silicon chip.

Voice Gram: A message like a telegram, but using the recorded voice rather than written words.

Voice Recognition Device: An input device, which allows a person to input data to a computer by speaking to it.

Voice Reproduction System: A voice response system, which produces audio output by selecting appropriate audio output from a set of pre-recorded audio responses.

Voice Response System: An output device, which enables a compute to talk to its users.

Voiceband: Data communications system, which handles moderate volumes of data, typically from 300 to 9600 bauds. Phone lines, which we use to talk to other people is an example.

VoIP (Voice Over IP): A term used for IP telephony. VoIP includes call setup and termination as well as the transmission of digitized audio.

Volatile Storage: A storage medium, which loses its contents when power fails, or when power is switched off.

VPI/VCI (Virtual Path Identifier/ Virtual Channel Identifier): A binary value used in an ATM network to identify a particular connection. Each switch along a path rewrites the VPI/VCI.

VPN (Virtual Private Network): A technology that uses encryption and IP tunneling to allow a multi-site organization to use low-cost Internet connections among sites but still keep data confidential.

VSAT (Very Small Aperture Terminal): An earth station which uses a very small diameter dish (1 to 2 metre) antenna to transmit and receive digital data from satellites.

VXML (Voice Extensible Markup Language): A markup language used for Web pages that contain audio (typically used with cell phones).

W

w3c/wwwc: Authority which makes policy decisions on world wide web.

WAN (Wide Area Network): A network that uses technology designed to span a large geographic area. For example, a satellite network is a WAN because a satellite can relay communication across an entire continent. WANs have higher propagation delay than LANs or MANs. See LAN and MAN.

Wand: A light pen attached to a point of sale unit used for reading bar codes.

WAP (Wireless Access Protocol): A set of protocols designed to deliver and display pages of information on small, portable wireless devices such as portable telephones and pagers.

Watermark: Faded picture placed at the background of a document.

3-way Handshake: A technique used by TCP and other transport protocols to reliably start or gracefully terminate communication.

WDM (Wavelength Division Multiplexing): A frequency division multiplexing technique applied to optical fiber.

WEB: Short form of 'world wide web'.

Web Browser: Software used to see webpages in HTML format.

Web Camera: A simple camera that can be plugged into a personal computer. It works by converting light into binary digits.

Web Client: Any computer on the Internet, which can access web servers.

Web Directory: Organization of web documents according to broad division of topics like Arts and Humanities, Sports, etc.

Web Page: A document written in Hyper Text Markup Language that can be seen through a browser programme like Netscape, Internet Explorer, etc.

Web Server: Any computer on the Internet, which uses the HTTP protocol.

Webmaster: A person skilled in creating and maintaining Web pages.

WEP (Wired Equivalency Privacy): The original privacy mechanism that was part of IEEE 802.11 wireless networks. WEP was found to be insufficient. See WPA.

Wide Area Network (WAN): A computer network, which interconnects computers spread over a large geographical area. It may also enable LANs to communicate with each other. This type of network may be developed to operate nationwide or worldwide, and the transmission medium used are normally public systems, such as telephone lines, microwave and satellite links.

Wi-Fi: A marketing term invented by an alliance of vendors who sell 802.11 wireless networking technology.

Wildcard (Character): A special character, usually a? or an *, which is used in software commands as a generic reference to any character, or any combination of characters, respectively.

Winchester Disk: Medium-sized, non-interchangeable metal disks permanently housed in sealed, contamination-free containers, with built-in read/write heads.

Window: A rectangular portion of a computer screen, which is dedicated to specific activity or application. The display screen can be separated into several windows to simultaneously show the status of the different applications at any instance of time.

Windows: An operating system developed by Microsoft for use on personal computers. Its various release versions are Windows 3.0, Windows 95, Windows 98, Windows 2000 and Windows XP.

Windows NT: A multi-user, timesharing operating system developed by Microsoft, which has Unix-like features. It is designed to be used for powerful workstations, and network and database servers.

Windows NT Operating System: A multi-user, multitasking portable OS designed by Microsoft for high end PCs used as servers.

3-wire Circuit: A wiring scheme often used with asynchronous serial connections between a pair of computers. The first wire is used to transmit data from one computer to another, the second wire is used to transmit data in the reverse direction, and the third wire is a common electrical ground.

Wireless LAN: A LAN in which a mobile computer such as a Laptop computer can send or receive messages to or from a base station connected to the LAN.

Wireless Markup Language (WML): The underlying computer code that produces pages that display on the wireless Web.

Wizard: A help tool (usually in step-by-step format) that steers the user through to completion of a task.

Wood Block: A method of printing, whereby the linked face of a carved wooden block is presented down onto paper.

Word: A sub-division of the central processor store containing a standard number of bits. It is individually addressable. Locations in the main memory are called words which are further sub-divided into smaller units called bytes.

Word Length: A measure of the size of a word, usually specified in units, such as characters or bits. Each location of a computer system can store a fixed number of characters or bits, called its word length.

Word Processing: The use of computers to create, view, edit, format, store, retrieve, and print text materials.

Word Processor: A computer programme which can perform fairly intensive numerical computation. Typical work stations use a powerful processor 10 to 100 times faster than PCs, 1 GB of main memory, 100 GB disk, and a 19 inch colour monitor. They use UNIX as their Operating System.

Word Wrap: A word processing feature, which automatically moves words down to the beginning of the next line, if they extend beyond the right margin.

Word-addressable Storage: Storage designed to store a fixed number of characters (equal to its word-length in bytes). For such a storage device, storage space is always allocated in multiples of word-length. Its another name is fixed-word-length storage.

WordArt: Special text effects in the word processor programme Word.

Work Area: Area on the screen where the user is currently carrying out his work.

Worksheet: A grid of rows and column, part of a workbook in a spreadsheet programme (like MS Excel).

Workstation: A powerful desktop computer designed to meet the computing needs of engineers, architects, and other professionals, who need greater processing power, larger storage, and better graphics display facility than what PCs provide.

World Wide Web (WWW or W3): Network of computers across the world interconnected together on the internet, and using the concept of hypertext to link internet sites and information on the internet.

Worm: A computer virus designed to erase/after the data/ programme from a computer system's memory/ disk.

WPA (Wi-Fi Protected Access): A replacement for WEP.

Write-Once, Read-Many (WORM) disk: An optical disk, which looks like a standard CD-ROM disk, but allows the user to record his/her own information on it by using a CD-recordable (CD-R) drive.

WYSIWYG: Stands for What You See Is What You Get. This feature of a word-processing package allows the users to display a document on the screen in a form, which closely resembles what the printed document will look like.

X

XCF: Format of picture files in Gimp.

XDR (External Data Representation): A standard used with RPC to allow heterogeneous computers to exchange character, integer, and floating point values.

XML (Extensible Markup Language): A markup language that is used primarily for exchange of data between two computer programmes. An XML document contains embedded tags that give names for fields in the data. Unlike HTML, XML does not specify formatting information.

XMMS: Software in GNU/Linux to hear sound.

Y

YACC: Yet Another Compiler Compiler is a programming tool which generates the parser for a high level language when the rules of syntax of the language are given.

Z

Zero Compression: A technique IPv6 uses to abbreviate hexadecimal colon notation by replacing a sequence of zeroes with a pair of colons.

.zip: File extension of a compressed file.

Zip: Reduce the size of a file (See Compression).

Zip Disk: See Bernoulli disk.

Zip Drive: A hardware for housing zip floppy. It can be attached to a computer. Data can be saved on zip floppy.

Zip File: A file that has been compressed using PKZIP or a similar programme.

Zipping: See Compression.

Zoned Decimal Number: Any numeric character coded in the Extended Binary Coded Decimal Interchange Code (EBCDIC). Each decimal digit occupies one byte of storage.

Zoom: The command to see a thing on the screen as enlarged or as reduced.

Bibliography

A. Freedman, *The Computer Glossary*, Prentice Hal, Inc. Englewood Cliffs, N.J., 1983.

A.S. Tanenbaum, *Computer Networks*, 2nd Ed., Prentice Hall of India (P) Ltd., New Delhi, 1981.

D.E. Comer, *Internetworking with TCP/IP*, Vol. I, Prentice Hall of India (P) Ltd., New Delhi, 1995.

D.L. Slotnick and J.K. Slotnick, *Computers; Their Structure, Use and Influence*, Prentice Hall, Inc., Englewood Cliffs, N.J., 1979.

J.F. Kurose, K.W. Ross. *Computer Networking*, Addison-Wesley Longman, 2001.

J. Frates and W. Moldrup, *Computers and Life*, Prentice Hall, Inc., Englewood Cliffs. N.J., 1983.

J. Martin, *Telecommunications and the Computer*, 3rd Ed., Prentice Hall of India (P) Ltd., New Delhi, 1990.

J.D. Foley, A. Van Dam, S.K. Feiner and J.F. Hughes, *Interactive Computer Graphics*, 2nd Ed., Addison- Wesley, Reading, Mass, 1996.

Jain. V.K. (2001). *Computer for Beginners*. New Delhi: Pustak Mahal.

Mallik. U. (2002). *Learning with Computers*. New Delhi: NCERT.

P.V.S. Rao, *Perspectives in Computer Architecture*, Prentice Hall of India (P) Ltd., New Delhi, 1992.

SCERT, Kerala. *Information Technology*, Standard X.

SCERT, Kerala. *Kerala Reader, Information Technology*, Standard IX.

SCERT, Kerala. *Kerala Reader, Information Technology*, Standard VIII.

Sinha, P.K., Sinha, P. (2003). *Computer Fundamentals* 3rd Ed. New Delhi, BPB Publications.

T. Viswanathan, *Telecommunication Switching Systems and Networks*, Prentice Hall of India (P) Ltd., New Delhi, 1992.

W.K. Giloi, *Interactive Computer Graphics*, Prentice Hall of India (P) Ltd. New Delhi, 1978.

W.M. Newman and R.F. Sproull, *Principles of Interactive Computer Graphics*, 2nd Ed., McGraw Hill Inc, New York, 1981.

W. Stallings, *Local Network*, 3rd Ed, Mc Millan, New York, 1990.